A Pocketful of Light

13 Days in Italy, the World's First Tourist Destination

A Pocketful of Light

13 Days in Italy, the World's First Tourist Destination

Jan Stafford Kellis

A POCKETFUL OF LIGHT. Copyright © 2011 by Jan Stafford Kellis. All rights reserved. Printed in the United States of America. No part of this book may be used or reproduced in any manner whatsoever without express written permission from the author except in the case of brief quotations embodied in critical articles and reviews. For information, address Myrno Moss Perspectives, Post Office Box 536, De Tour Village, MI 49725.

All interior photographs copyright © 2011 by Jan Stafford Kellis.

Front cover artwork copyright © 2011 by Jan Stafford Kellis.

ISBN 978-1461187493

Dedication

This book is for Stephanie, my daughter and
favorite traveling companion.
Ti amo. Buona fortuna, figlia!

ALSO BY JAN STAFFORD KELLIS

FICTION

The Word That You Heard

NONFICTION

Bookworms Anonymous:
A Non-Traditional Book Club for Every Reader

A Word From the Author

Italy has always fascinated me: the culture, the cuisine, the fashion, the history, the art. When I started researching Italy as a travel destination, my first Google search revealed Rick Steves' *Italy 2010,* ready to confirm I'd chosen the perfect vacation spot. His tips, suggestions and warnings provided enough information for me to envision my entire thirteen-day stay; I consulted his website (www.ricksteves.com) and read other travelers' stories to collect tips and caveats, determined to provide my daughter with the perfect Italian tour.

Our trip begins in Venice, the iconic city most people envision when they hear the word Italy. The gondolas, the canals, the bridges. So foreign and yet so familiar, it's the perfect starting point for our Italian immersion.

From there, we ride the Trenitalia to Siena and take day-trips to Florence, Volterra and San Gimignano. Our next stayover is in Sorrento where we explore the Amalfi Coast before hitting Rome for two and a half days.

It's a grand adventure; my research began eighteen months before our departure. We learned basic Italian so we could converse with the locals, and we packed everything in a carry-on backpack (purchased from Rick Steves' website) to make relocating easier. I've included some photos of the trip so you can see what we saw.

Tourists have visited Italy since ancient Roman times, when they traveled to attend events at the Colosseum, earning Italy the reputation as the world's first tourist destination.

Come along on our journey—see, smell, hear, taste and experience Italy with us. There are a few simple Italian phrases littered throughout, so I've included a glossary in the back of the book to assist you if needed. Feel free to use any or all of our itinerary ideas for your own trip.

Ciao!

Explanation of Chapter Numeration

Leonardo Fibonacci of Pisa, mathematically instrumental to the evolution of physics, engineering and astronomy, discovered a numbering sequence present throughout nature. This sequence revealed the patterns found in hurricanes, sunflowers, DNA molecules and galaxies in outer space. The Fibonacci Sequence, then, explains many natural phenomena. In honor of his contributions to our daily lives (he also pioneered the use of Arabic numbers—without Mr. Fibonacci, we'd still be calculating with Roman numerals!) I have numbered the chapters in this book according to his famous Golden Ratio.

Can you find the pattern in Fibonacci's numbers? To confirm your answer, check the appendix.

Disclaimer

This book is intended to inspire you to travel and explore foreign cultures; it is not a guarantee, implicit or explicit, of happy or even satisfactory adventures. I hope your trip is just as fabulous as ours was, and this book may well improve your odds.

The purpose of this book is to educate and entertain. The author and Myrno Moss Perspectives shall have neither liability nor responsibility to any person or entity with respect to any loss or damage caused or alleged to be caused directly or indirectly by the information presented in this book.

If you do not wish to be bound by the above, you may return this book to the publisher for a full refund.

Benvenuto in Italia! Welcome to Italy, land of wonder, old-world hostess, original vacation destination. I spent eighteen months researching Italy and lost myself in its myriad facets, its numerous incongruent personalities. While I can't claim expert status on any one subject, I am casually acquainted with much of Italy's culture and a smidgeon of its history and language.

A Venetian doorway

Table of Contents

Chapter 0, Preparation: Architecture of a Vacation	13
Chapter 1, Day One: Arriving in Venezia	27
Chapter 1, Day Two: Venezia	37
Chapter 2, Day Three: Venezia	51
Chapter 3, Day Four: Firenze, Siena	61
Chapter 5, Day Five: Siena	71
Chapter 8, Day Six: San Gimignano, Volterra	79
Chapter 13, Day Seven: Siena	97
Chapter 21, Day Eight: Sorrento by Rail	111
Chapter 34, Day Nine: Sorrento, Positano	127
Chapter 55, Day Ten: Sorrento	137
Chapter 89, Day Eleven: Pompeii, Roma	149
Chapter 144, Day Twelve: Roma	165
Chapter 233, Day Thirteen: Roma	173
Chapter 377, Later: Maintaining Perspective	193
Appendix	203

Entry to Harry's Bar

Chapter Zero
The Architecture of a Vacation

Questo è come il cacio sui maccheroni.
This is like cheese on macaroni.
(This is just what the doctor ordered.)

I harbor obsessive tendencies over things large and small. Usually these tendencies are somewhat congruent with my personality, but every now and then I fall victim to a startlingly unanticipated whim and sweep myself away in pursuit of new shoes or pretty ribbons. I also love to travel, and suffer from an uncontrollable destination obsession. If a friend mentions a place they've visited or plan to visit, or someone they know may visit, or a place that may or may not even exist, my fingers start Googling. The maps, tourist convention bureaus and demographic information fascinate me. Pretty soon I'm checking flights against my calendar and weighing my remaining vacation time, envisioning myself in the Bahamas sipping mai tais or in Omaha eating steak.

Then I remember I don't like the heat. And I don't eat meat. I sigh, thinking what a great trip it might have been.

Gradually I become aware of my surroundings again and realize I've been part of a conversation about a trip my friend went on fifteen years ago, before New Orleans flooded, before SARS and Swine flu and 9/11. At this point, to justify my crazed demeanor and recent mad typing, I regale said friend with current statistics, flight information and a couple of recommended hotels in the area. This is usually when the subject is changed suddenly and severely, leaving me with yet another unfulfilled vacation dream (it's usually enough for me to vacation vicariously, but my friends frequently throw destination names around without realizing I'm like a dog watching a raw steak sailing by my nose; and then they don't even take the trip! They were truly just *making conversation*!).

I try to curb my travel enthusiasm to preserve marital harmony and address budget restrictions, but my wanderlust sometimes reconnoiters my common sense and I find myself drooling on maps and feverishly calculating and recalculating food and hotel costs, measuring them against my discretionary income and projecting the growth of my travel savings account. I revisit the websites and reread their promises: exciting adventures, activities, sights, shopping. If I close my eyes I can picture myself there, on the town square, surveying my shopping opportunities and eating lunch before attending the live performance or climbing to the top of the bell tower.

About eighteen months ago, one of my co-workers mentioned her recent trip to Italy and told me how fabulous the country was: the people were friendly, the scenery beautiful, the food phenomenal. And the history! "You can't believe it until you see it," she said.

"Oh no," I thought. I felt a shift in my posture, as if my travel bone had suddenly clicked into place. "I'm going," I said aloud.

"What? Where?" asked my co-worker. She'd been telling me about their tour guide and their daily schedule and how to harvest olives in Italy (there are three ways, which I'll explain later). She clearly hadn't noticed my travel bone shifting into place.

"To Italy. I'm going—probably in a year or two." *This is how an obsession is born,* I thought. *This is what a fresh obsession looks like, all shiny and sparkly. Mesmerizing.*

"Okay," she laughed. "Well, let me know if you need any tour information."

"Sure, send it to my office." Besides being a part-time obsessive, I'm an information junkie and a control engineer. I knew I wouldn't go on a tour but wanted to view their itineraries and possibly steal ideas from them.

Obviously a journey half way around the world deserves at least two weeks' time, and should incorporate at least half of the country, feature both urban and rural destinations and include plenty of touristy sights as well as obscure discoveries. My first concern is always tourist season itself: I like to avoid the crowds, and always plan our vacations during the "low" season.

My husband wasn't interested in going to a foreign country where he didn't speak the language and wouldn't know exactly how his food was prepared, so I informed my daughter Stephanie she would be accompanying me to Italy. My grandiose vacation plans didn't impress her for one second: "Why Italy?" she asked, wrinkling her nose. At fifteen she'd ceased being awed or overwhelmed by anything, but I still occasionally expected a reaction stronger than apathy.

"It's a cool country. You'll see, we'll have a great time. We'll be gone two weeks, but it'll be over spring break so you'll miss a week of school."

"*Two weeks?* Mom, that's way too long. I can only go for one week."

"We're going for two. I'm not traveling across the globe for one tiny week." We had this same conversation approximately nine hundred times before the trip, and three hundred times during the trip. Like a comedy act after our millionth performance, we recited lines by rote without any emotion or awareness of our audience. I now realize I could have avoided immeasurable frustration had I recorded it and simply pressed 'play' every time she started the sequence.

My Italy file grew quickly. Bulging with maps and printouts of traveler comments and cautions, restaurant recommendations and sightseeing strategies, the file proved ineffective and I realized I needed a new strategy to handle the research for such a long, diverse trip. Previously I'd planned for trips lasting four to nine days, road trips in the US or Canada with no language barrier or culture shock (the time we visited Tennessee we suffered a mild culture reaction but not a true shock). To properly prepare for the Italy trip, I needed to begin with a broader perspective and determine first which cities we would visit, then which activities or sights we would include in our ironclad itinerary, and which we would keep on our contingent itinerary in case we found ourselves with surplus money, time and energy.

Instead of a file, the Italy trip required a special section in my day planner notebook (see my notes regarding the notebook I created in the appendix) with a page or two for each part of the trip. Page one of the notebook section labeled Italy listed every consideration specific to this trip:

Language (the only Italian words I knew were lasagna and spaghetti)
Culture differences
Communication (calling home from abroad is $3/minute! I needed an affordable alternative)
Passports (we didn't have any)
Budget and savings plan
Electrical issues (Europe uses a higher voltage than the US)
Luggage (backpack or rolling suitcase?)
Transportation within Italy (Trains or buses?)
Lodging (Hostels or hotels? Or bed and breakfasts?)
Schedule (how long in each city? I wanted to stay in at least four cities)

I like to compare the research phase of trip planning to the honeymoon phase of a relationship: Everything is still ideal, nothing has gone wrong yet and perfection is attainable. One has only to conceive every possible circumstance or contingency and plan accordingly, and the shimmer of a flawless journey makes excellence seem a reasonable expectation. The anticipation energizes me by day and interrupts my sleep at night, causing me to wake up and jot down cryptic phrases to consider in the morning. Train schedules; tipping waiters; negotiating etiquette at street markets.

When the alarm clock sounded I'd been awake for an hour anticipating its summons. My head stuffed and ears ringing from the virus I'd been unable to shake, I thought to myself: *the next time I wake up, I'll be in Italy.* My backpack stood ready as it had for the past two weeks, when I could no longer wait to fill it with clothes, schedules, pre-purchased tickets, electrical outlet adaptors and a quart-sized bag of allowable liquids for the flight. Stephanie had packed her bag the night before and it was suspiciously light and empty looking.

My right hand ring finger was swollen, cracked and bleeding and I was reluctant to expose it to the germs we'd collect on the plane. A frantic search yielded a four-year expired package of liquid bandage—perfect for sealing the cracks to prevent germs from entering. My finger breaks out like this every spring and fall and I've taken it to a couple of dermatologists and several doctors, but the cream they prescribe never seems to repair the problem.

"Should I use this stuff? It expired in 2006."

"It'll be fine," my husband answered, breaking the top off the bottle as he opened it for me. "Hmm. It was glued shut. This stuff doesn't really go bad, does it?"

I shrugged and covered my cracked and bleeding finger with it, one eye on the clock. We said our good-byes and reviewed the communication options one last time before Steph and I loaded our bags in the truck and rolled out of the driveway.

Driving to the airport, a four-hour trip, allowed time for me to realize after all the months of preparation and anticipation, of studying Italian, researching hotels and sights and gleaning tips and information from other travelers, we were finally at the threshold of our trip. It was like my practical exam and I hoped I'd properly prepared for everything. The liquid bandage on my finger remained sticky; about halfway to the airport I tired of picking lint from it and wrapped a band-aid around it.

We flew from the Lansing Regional Airport, a friendly little place with free WiFi and an accommodating staff who offered help at each step. It had been eleven years since Steph had flown and she had no real memory of it. Neither of us had flown so far or on such a large plane before (except when my parents moved back to the USA from Australia, where I was born, but I was only two years old at the time).

We easily navigated the Detroit Metro Airport and hopped on the plane to Amsterdam, taking our seats by the window. The eight-hour flight was the first chance I'd had in days to truly relax and allow my mind to catch up to my body. The previous morning we'd all risen early to drive our other daughter, Dani, recently separated from her boyfriend and at loose ends, to a nearby airport to put her on a plane to Alaska. The plan was for her to stay with my aunt and find a summer job, then decide what to do next. She was only twenty years old but I felt like she was floundering around in the forest of life with no compass and changing the scenery out her window just might provide the direction she needed. It was heartbreaking flying in opposite directions, and the ten-hour time difference would make communicating difficult. By the time our plane left Lansing, Dani had arrived in Juneau, spent the night in a hotel, and was heading north on the ferry to Haines.

Dani was born free of artifice and continually surprised us with her creative translations of life events. Although her face revealed every thought and opinion she held, her sunny-side-up optimism carried her through most travails. Sometimes it seemed we'd grown up together, I was so young and unprepared for her arrival. She'd inherited her dad's blonde hair and my slight build, but her eyes are colored deeper than either of ours: an arresting sapphire blue. The last time we'd seen her, brave expression pasted in place as she wheeled her new luggage through the terminal, kept invading my thoughts.

The plane flew on as I monitored our progress across the Atlantic Ocean. Unable to concentrate on a movie or even the printed page of my book, I resorted to brief magazine articles and occasional video games on my iPhone when my mind grew restless again. Steph watched movies and played games on the video screen on the back of the seat in front of her, marveling at the relative comfort of our seats and the meals and snacks served during the flight. She brought a Nintendo DS game along but since we didn't have a voltage converter for it we planned to buy one at our first stop.

We gazed at Manchester (I think), a puddle of lights in the vast pre-dawn darkness, the first sign of life we'd seen since reaching the ocean off the coast of Canada.

Touching down in Amsterdam at 5:30 a.m. local time offered a clear view of the sleeping city, its intricate pattern of canals and streets presenting an intriguing picture. My wanderlust awakened, I regretted not trying a little harder to arrange a layover in Amsterdam on our way to Venice. Then I decided I'd rather not use our Italy time up here in the Netherlands—exploring Amsterdam would have to belong to a future trip.

The Amsterdam-Schipohl Airport is larger than it seems. The announcements on the PA system were first communicated in a harsh, clumsy Dutch followed by an English version, quite melodious when spoken with a Dutch accent. We explored the shops, opening for the day an hour after we arrived, and decided to have a snack at the lunch counter. My money was carefully separated by destination, each packet labeled with a city name or the word 'hotels' to increase the odds it would last as long as I'd planned. The different sizes of the Euros are awkward to handle and this being my first purchase, the smallest bill I had was a fifty. I smiled an apology to the counter man as I handed it to him for my €5,76 purchase, unprepared for his reaction.

"Fifty Euros?" He yelled out, as if announcing a bid at an auction. "You must be rich!"

"No, no!" we shook our heads, eyes round, hands extended to eradicate this idea from the air as soon as he uttered it. "It's all we have."

"Aah, this is all," he grinned at our anxiety. I shoved the change he handed me in my front pocket, unwilling to open my purse again and risk exposing the wad of money tucked in there.

We sat facing opposite directions so we could easily observe the other patrons and the counter. Steph seemed nervous after our first foreign interaction, and I felt rattled as I considered my responsibility for my daughter as well as myself. I wondered how much reading travelers' tales of woe was helping and how much it increased my paranoia, hearing about people whose cameras were stolen from around their necks without their knowledge or people who arrived at their hotels with empty suitcase pockets, the thieves emptying them as the travelers wheeled the bags behind them, unaware they were being followed let alone robbed.

The remaining time at the Amsterdam airport passed without incident—we searched in vain for a magazine printed in English for Steph and I received a text message from home saying a store in Oregon had just ordered three copies of Bookworms Anonymous, my first book, its sales remaining steady since publication. A new store's interest in my book was always welcome news.

After admiring our first passport stamps in the Amsterdam-Schipohl Airport, we boarded our last flight to Venice. This flight boasted no video screens, but the announcements were delivered in two languages just like they were in the airport: Dutch, followed by English. Every flight attendant spoke fluent English, explaining various safety precautions and serving pastries stuffed with marmalade and cream cheese.

So far, everyone we encountered spoke English. I half-hoped I wouldn't need my skeletal Italian vocabulary and half-hoped I would, wishing I'd practiced charades recently just in case.

Gondola ready for passengers

Chapter One
Arriving in Venezia
sabato (Saturday)

Togliti dai piedi!
Take yourself out of my feet!
(Get out of the way!)

Immediately overwhelming. Chaotic, confusing and, well, foreign. My first impressions of Venezia were compromised by one of my best assets, my self-confidence, as it took a few minutes to realize and then admit I had no idea how to get where I needed to go.

Then I remembered the travel information booklet I'd made. A quick consultation reminded me we had to first locate the ticket office to buy a bus ticket to the Venezia station, then we'd be able to walk from there to our hotel.

The ticket office was easy to find but the ticket

agent spoke no English. Her gestures were so confusing we ended up going back upstairs, then down again before locating the exit (labeled *uscita*, showing a little man running toward a door) and racing out to wait at the platform. We had only ten minutes to wait before the next bus; plenty of time to remind each other we were now breathing Italian air (it smelled like a city, surprise surprise) and read the sign indicating the bus departure times every few seconds to assure ourselves we were standing in the right spot.

"It stinks here," Steph wrinkled her nose and nodded toward a cluster of people smoking cigarettes.

"It'll smell better when we reach Venice. Have I told you about the olive harvest? There are three ways to harvest olives."

"No, Mom," she rolled her eyes and glanced around. Finding no other distraction, she said, "okay, what are the three ways?"

"Well, you can shake the trees really hard and let the olives fall, then rake them up."

"Mmmhmm."

"Or, you can physically pluck the olives from the branches."

"This is fascinating, Mom."

"Or, you can lay down a blanket, open a bottle of Chianti and wait for the olives to fall." I waited for a reaction. "Isn't that cool? Just have a picnic and the olives will come to you."

"Yes, that is very cool. Oh good, here's our

bus."

The bus ride provided enough time for me to scan the map of Venice one last time, fixing our location and our destination in my head so I wouldn't have to refer to it at every step once we debarked from the bus.

We set off in the general direction of our hotel and continued until we found the intersection we needed, then walked right past the door to our hotel. It was more of a bed and breakfast, its portal a regular-sized door with no awning or other characteristics to mark it as a commercial establishment. I first noticed the chocolate shop across the street, which I'd listed in my written directions, and when I looked at the nondescript door to our bed and breakfast it took a minute to notice the tiny brass plaque reading 'Al Campaniel'. We'd found it!

The door was locked.

After ringing the doorbell a few times with an increasingly anxious tempo, I read the sign directing those whose rings aren't answered to walk around the corner to the pay phone and call a toll-free number. Steph didn't want to carry her bag another inch, but I wasn't about to let her out of my sight. "Not a chance, ladybug. We have to stick together," I told her. We hoisted our backpacks up again and found the pay phone. Marco answered on the second ring and assured us he would send Jacqueline over to let us in within ten minutes.

We schlepped our bags back to the hotel door and dropped them wearily at our feet. I wondered how we'd be able to carry these bags for two weeks if we were tired on the first day.

An elderly man interrupted my thoughts when he stopped on the street and pointed to us, grinning, "Bella, Bella! Sorelli?" he pointed from me to Steph and back again. "Sorelli?" We shrugged and looked at each other, then I remembered the Italian word for sister: *sorella*. Changing the last vowel to an 'i' makes an Italian word plural. He was asking if we were sisters! I shook my head no and he said, "Aaah, mama, figlia. Bella, bella." *Mother, daughter. Beautiful, beautiful.* He kissed his fingers and flung the kisses toward us, then continued along the narrow street and rounded the corner.

Jacqueline arrived as promised, a trim and tiny lady with a long gray braid, speaking quietly and punctuating every sentence with a smile. She spoke very little English but was fluent in French and Italian, so by speaking very slowly we were able to untangle the codes of our various languages. Our room on the second floor contained twin beds, two comfortable chairs and a desk and chair. We had a private bathroom as well, with a shower and a lovely warming towel rack. The toilet was a mystery at first, but we figured out how to flush it within minutes: by pressing the large plastic panel about three feet above the stool itself. Gratefully flopping on the beds, we allowed ourselves a brief rest before venturing out. Our shoulders and backs already felt tender from lugging our heavy backpacks and we needed this respite.

Nearly every time I'd searched for Venice restaurants on the Internet a link to Harry's Bar popped up. I'd read the story several times about Harry Cipriani establishing his tiny little bar and inventing his signature drink, the Peach Bellini, which he served to an exclusive clientele of royalty, celebrities and others with well-lined pockets. Harry's Bar quickly shot to the top of my list of must-sees, as the descriptions alone drew me in and made me long to experience this famous place. I'd mapped out two routes to Harry's from our hotel, so we could cross the Grand Canal via the Rialto Bridge on our way there and the Accademia Bridge on our way back, no backtracking required. We were hungry by the time we left our room, but I insisted on waiting until we found Harry's Bar, sure it would be a dinner we'd always remember. After eating there, of course, we remembered it for entirely different reasons than I'd supposed.

Harry's is situated just off Piazza San Marco, or St. Mark's Square, the most famous square in Venezia, right along the Grand Canal. We walked right past it without noticing the subtle gold lettering on the window humbly proclaiming HARRY'S BAR. After inquiring at the next restaurant and being directed back to it, we entered through the narrow door into a cozy diner-style restaurant with a bar lining one side. The waitress greeted us in Italian, but was quick to notice our confusion and revised in English: Drink, or eat?

"Eat," I motioned eating as if with a fork. She signaled a waiter who seated us in a corner booth and gave us menus.

The prices were shockingly high. I didn't want to offend these people, having just entered their country, but I longed to get up and run out the door. Looking back now I realize they probably would have been glad to see us go, responding with a shake of the head and a brusque "crazy Americana." Silently reminding myself I would most likely never grace Harry's doorstep again, I decided to redeem the situation by choosing carefully from the menu and enjoying the meal. As Steph and I whispered different options, the man at the next table leaned toward us and said sotto voce, "you can split an entrée. They don't advertise it, but they allow it."

"Oh, thanks for telling us! We weren't really prepared for these prices," I said.

"We weren't either. We're hoping every restaurant isn't like this."

We chose the spinach ricotta ravioli, clumsily conveying to the waiter our wish to split one order through a combination of charades and the Italian words for "one" and "two". I also ordered my much anticipated and coveted Peach Bellini, which came in a short, squat glass about the size of a jigger. The waiter delivered our order, neatly divided and presented on two plates. There were no side dishes except the bread on the table. Our meal consisted of a piece of bread and eight thin homemade ravioli each and of course a sip of Peach Bellini, for €63,20 or approximately $92.91. This alarming figure was only €7 short of our daily food budget and we'd eaten only one meal.

We left Harry's Bar still hungry and slightly dispirited, but the carnival atmosphere of Venezia quickly revived us as we meandered through Piazza San Marco past the accordion and cello players, wending our way through crowds of European and American tourists. The warnings I'd read and heard from other travelers played like a loop tape in my head; I didn't take my eyes from Steph for more than a few seconds at a time, just long enough to verify the direction we were heading was the correct one. We headed toward the Accademia Bridge to avoid retracing our steps back to our hotel. The trick in Venezia is to walk in the general direction in which one wishes to go, allowing for the frequent detours necessary due to the configuration of the small connecting streets and bridges. When one is close to the targeted destination, it's time to pay attention to the street names and choose the correct ones.

From above, the pedestrians must resemble rats in a labyrinth as they scurry along the corridor-like Venetian streets, occasionally turning back when encountering a dead end.

We located our hotel again after enjoying a brief performance by a man making music by rubbing wine glass rims with his fingers. I'd heard this before, of course, but not so complicated a tune. He was actually playing classical music, using two or three glasses at a time to create sophisticated sounds. Steph announced she was already homesick and demanded time for a nap before we continued exploring, so we collapsed in our room for an hour or two. It was 3pm in Venice—four hours after we'd arrived in the city, and 27 hours after we had left home that morning.

I hoped I wasn't killing what little wanderlust she'd inherited by dragging her across the globe on a trip she'd neither asked for nor shown any interest in taking.

After a brief nap, Steph rallied and we wandered around our immediate neighborhood, shopping and stopping for a bruschetta snack at the corner bar. In Italian, it's pronounced broo-sket-ta, rather than broo-shet-ta as is customary in the States. The simple bread, tomato and cheese snack was restorative and satisfying, and only cost €10,50 with a bottle of water. I promised myself I'd stop dwelling on the disappointment and disenchantment of Harry's Bar, and use it as a learning experience.

We turned in for the night around 8pm, both of us exhausted from traveling and attempting to navigate and communicate. By that time we'd been awake for thirty-two hours, traveled 4,576 miles by air, fifteen miles by bus and five miles on foot. My eyes were closing even as I tried to send a text message home to assure my husband we were in for the night, safe and sound.

One would expect the streets of Venezia, free of motorized vehicles, to be silent at night, but the sounds keeping us awake were comprised of people calling to each other, high heels clipping by on the stone street and travelers wheeling their suitcases past the door. The architecture of Venezia's streets, with their tall stone walls, amplify even the tiniest sounds. We slept fitfully our first night.

A narrow Venetian canal

Chapter One
Exploring Venezia
domenica (Sunday)

Non so che pesci pigliare.
I don't know which fish to catch.
(I don't know what to do first/where to start.)

I have an irrational fear of mice. I realize it's irrational, but I'm terrified. So terrified, in fact, I don't allow myself to imagine what will happen when I encounter one. Although, maybe realistically imagining the weak little mouse's reaction, most likely seeking escape in the other direction, might cure my fear. Mice are sneaky, dirty, germ-carrying vermin. They make me nauseous. One night as I was drifting off to sleep at home, my husband Jason snoring beside me, my daughter opened our door and announced, "there's a mouse in the bathroom." Jason, unconcerned, managed to stand upright and pursue the intruder, who ran out of the bathroom right past our bedroom door. This was before an eye surgeon resurrected my vision and, in a myopic moment of sheer terror, the mouse appeared about the size of my foot, a gray furry blur sprinting past the doorway as I lay rigid under the covers, recently re-tucked so I resembled a lumpy mummy. Jason cornered the mouse and euthanized it somehow—I never ask for details about these encounters—and returned to bed, snoozing again as soon as he was horizontal.

I remained awake all night long, straining my ears for tiny squeaks or scurrying noises that would indicate the arrival of the mouse's relatives and friends, most likely already established in the basement and building a little mouse ramp to access our main floor and feast on dog food and stray crumbs. When I awakened Steph the next morning I discovered her primitive mouse barrier, a large blanket stuffed under the door, which allowed her to rest easily throughout the night. If I'd thought of blocking off our door I probably still wouldn't have slept for worry about what I'd see when I opened the door in the morning.

As I said, this fear is irrational but nonetheless consuming, canceling any intellectual understanding I possess about mice and their inability and disinterest in attacking humans. (*But what if there were hundreds of mice at once, crawling and biting and spreading mouse germs?* My subconscious asks before I can shift my focus.)

As terrifying as mice are, rats are a hundred times more alarming with their larger size and aggressive behavior and their proclivity for living in sewer pipes. Venezia, known for its state of elegant decay, its proud bell tower and Doge's Palace on Piazza San Marco and its thousands of pigeons, is also a haven for rats. I stumbled upon rat-related comments from travelers during my initial research phase and the rat population almost prevented me from adding Venezia to our itinerary. If our trip had been planned during high rat season, we may have missed Venezia altogether, but in late March/early April the rats aren't as brave as they are during the summer months, yet not as hungry as they are during winter months. Our chances for seeing a rat during our vacation were quite slim. I believe in facing my fears occasionally, especially the irrational ones, so Venezia remained on our schedule, first on the list, my logic being if we saw a rat, we wouldn't have a worse experience during the remainder of our trip. And I'd prove to myself I could survive a rat encounter.

After arriving in Venezia and strolling through the labyrinthine streets, the possibility of encountering a rat (some reported seeing rats eighteen inches long, not counting the tail!) never left my mind. I hadn't told Steph about the rat issue, unwilling to add to her list of reasons for not enjoying our vacation, so I alone carried the burden of constantly vigilant rat patrol.

We never saw a rat, or even a mouse. I silently

congratulated myself for braving the streets of Venezia.

Rising early the next morning, we climbed from our room on the second floor to the dining room on the third floor, referred to as the 2nd *piano*, or level. Italians refer to the ground floor as zero, and one floor up is called the 1st *piano*, or level, while the basement is referred to as -1 *piano*. The dining room featured a rooftop patio with views of other rooftops but we chose a table inside as the morning was too chilly for dining al fresco.

Jacqueline bustled to our table with large glasses of blood orange juice and asked softly, "corn flakes or Muesli? Croissant, fruit, toast?" I ordered Muesli and coffee and Steph asked for toast. "Coffee served after," Jacqueline explained, returning to the kitchen.

She returned with our food, artfully presented on various platters and baskets: croissants, warmed and dusted with powdered sugar, three kinds of preserves, Nutella, cream cheese and dry toast, barely ¼" thick, and my bowl of Muesli. Only after I finished my cereal and set the bowl aside was I presented with a cup of coffee, strong and steaming but only half full. When I requested more coffee Jacqueline smiled and poured two gulps into the cup, explaining this was enough coffee for breakfast.

I flashed back on Rick Steves' admonition to leave the States behind and embrace the Italian culture and all of its differences. My habit at home is to drink two or three cups of coffee in the morning and another one or two in the afternoon, part of the satisfaction embodied in clutching the cup in my hands while socializing at work or reading on the weekend. I knew I wouldn't suffer a caffeine-withdrawal-induced headache as long as I drank at least one cup of strong coffee per day, but I missed the ritual itself.

We asked Jacqueline about the Doge's Palace: is it worth visiting? Our Rick Steves guidebook ranks it as a must-see sight. "If you visit Venezia, but you do not see the Doge's Palace," she shrugged, "you have not seen Venezia."

As we left the hotel with a loose plan consisting of wandering the streets until we reached Piazza San Marco and touring the Doge's Palace, we realized the streets were jampacked with people again. Steph quickly learned the pattern of the streets nearest our hotel, confidently navigating a quarter-mile radius around corners and through *piazzas* and *sotoportegi* (tunnels). I recognized our neighborhood streets but maintained only a general sense of the direction in which our hotel was from any given location. While out walking I generally had a map of the city in one hand, my camera in the other hand and my purse slung around my body, hanging from my left shoulder and bouncing on my right hip.

Market stalls were set up in the middle of the wider streets near the Rialto Bridge, tempting us with scarves in every color, purses made from soft, buttery Italian leather, Venetian masks and Murano glass products.

After examining wine bottle stoppers featuring a Murano glass ornament, I stopped at a stall to choose gifts for my sister and mother. The seller was immediately attentive, pointing out various designs, asking me which colors I like. I spied one with a square top, clear with gold ribbons running through it, that appeared to have a broken corner. As I reached for it the proprietor picked it up and deftly covered the corner with his thumb.

"Quanto costa?" I asked. How much does it cost?

"Sei," he responded, holding up six fingers.

I pointed at the one he held. "That one is broken," I pantomimed breaking a stick into two pieces.

"No, ees fine. Ees good. Sei Euro." The thumb remained clamped down on the broken corner. His grin filled his face but didn't reach his eyes and I was reminded fleetingly of Dopey, one of the seven dwarfs.

"No," I said, touching his thumb. "Broken." I pried his thumb up to reveal the broken corner while he feigned surprise, gasping and theatrically covering his mouth, his eyebrows shooting toward his hairline.

I don't know why, but I bought four wine bottle stoppers from him, inspecting each one closely and trying to jiggle the glass loose to ensure it wasn't about to fall apart. I left the broken one on the table.

We continued on our way, pausing at every market stall while Steph tried on various scarves and I opened purses, hanging them on my shoulder to test the fit. Our search for a voltage converter proved to be more difficult and time-consuming than we'd anticipated: no grocery store or general store carried such an item.

By the time we reached the Doge's Palace the line of visitors extended down the entire wall facing the Grand Canal and it moved painfully slow. We decided to return the next day at opening time so we could avoid the line. The bell tower featured a similar line despite the scaffolding, stacked up and draped with tarps to hide the workers as they repaired the exterior walls.

Turning down a narrow *calle* (street) to escape the hordes of people, we ended up on a circuitous route toward the Accademia Bridge where we planned to find and tour the Leonardo da Vinci museum. Allowing the position of the sun to maintain my sense of direction, we wandered aimlessly until we stumbled upon a restaurant showcasing fresh seafood on ice beds behind plate glass windows along the street. The informational placards. He'd devised various machines of torture, pulleys, the original bicycle design, a primitive hang glider, and of course he'd painted The Last Supper and the famous drawing of human anatomy. A replica of each of his most famous inventions or designs is featured within the museum. During the remainder of our trip we would see at least three other da Vinci museums, but this was the only one we visited.

The Guggenheim Museum, located not too far from the da Vinci display, was on our list of sights but it waited in the opposite direction of our hotel. We decided to skip it for now and return the next day, but somehow on the next day, our last in Venezia, the Guggenheim was forgotten and we never did see it, placing it at the top of our list of sights we missed— our list of regrets and disappointments.

We spent the remainder of the day walking and shopping, taking photos and remarking on the green and brown Rapunzel-esque algae tresses adorning the sides of every canal. As we walked and shopped I started picking out words and loosely translating conversations between people speaking rapid-fire Italian. "They're looking for a sale on shoes," I whispered to Steph, nodding toward two women as I decoded about 30 percent of their exchange and filled in the rest with my imagination.

I'd never taken a foreign language course in school; my grandfather, who'd been raised in Rumania and France when his father was a foreign diplomat, had started to teach me basic French but we never progressed beyond simple nouns and adjectives.

Learning Italian, while daunting at first, appealed to my sense of structure when I discovered the spelling and pronunciation rules don't allow exceptions like the English language has. In Italian, one can figure out how to spell a word after hearing it aloud, and one can likewise know what a word sounds like when reading it for the first time. For example, every time a word features a c followed by an i, the c is pronounced 'ch'. I use the word *ciao* to remember this rule. There are no exceptions. Most multi-syllabic words carry the emphasis on the next to last syllable.

My ability to recognize scattered words and decode portions of conversations inspired an interest in the language for Steph, who'd been apathetic at best about learning it with me, leaving me to listen to CDs and read phrase books on my own. I also made a set of flashcards featuring what I considered the most necessary words and tested myself on my new word retention for three months before our trip.

Attempting to design my own foreign language course I floundered, bouncing between studying pronunciation and basic nouns, commonly used phrases and words I figured I'd need to recognize on store signs or road signs so we'd be able to navigate. My new vocabulary words swam circles in my head, larger words munching smaller ones, swirling crazily and losing their attachments and references to English like so much Italian flotsam. *Buongiorno, sorella, donna, Americana, per favore, oggi.*

We stumbled upon our hotel almost by accident, not realizing we were already in our own neighborhood. Venezia is surprisingly small, each corridor-street only a few yards long between intersections or piazzas.

My finger itched beneath the bandage. I peeled it off expecting the finger to be nearly healed, gasping aloud at the alarming algae-green tinge. I left the finger unbandaged and reminded myself I was already on strong antibiotics for my head cold, vowing not to panic for another few days.

Steph and I lay in our respective twin beds, pushed together to suggest a large double bed, separated only by the bedspreads tucked in between us. We listened to passersby and chatted with our eyes closed.

"Buona notte, figlia," I whispered. Good night, daughter.

"Buona notte, mamma," she answered.

Interesting Venetian doorway

Chapter Two
Last Day in Venezia
lunedi (Monday)

Non ti perdere in un bicchier d'acqua.
Don't get lost in a glass of water
(Don't make a mountain out of a mole hill.)

We dedicated our last day in Venezia to water travel, purchasing a Vaporetto ticket at the closest tabacchi shop after breakfast and boarding at the San Toma stop around the corner from our Hotel. The ubiquitous tabacchi shops compare to American convenience stores. They are generally squashed into a space about ten by twenty feet square and offer cramped displays of products from tourist knick knacks to batteries, disposable cameras, cold drinks and transportation tickets. If a traveler needs something and isn't sure where to look, the tabacchi shop will either have it or will know where to get it. Tabacchi shops offer a combination of travelers' aid, information and keepsakes. Most tabacchi store clerks speak basic English.

Floating along the Grand Canal freshened our view of the city, as many of the facades are impossible to view from land. The phrase 'elegant decay' reverberated in my mind as I noted the palaces with their lowest floors barely above the water line. I'd read about the people living in some of these dwellings—unable to procure building permits to renovate their homes in a timely manner, they end up moving upstairs and sacrificing the canal-level *piano* to use only as an entrance. Venezia is famous for its snarled construction permitting processes, attempting to maintain the historical integrity without compromising the entire structure. It's an architectural conundrum and Nature won't wait for man's solution, steadily eroding the foundations of the finest Venetian palaces.

The Vaporetti system is efficient and cost effective—Venezia's answer to the traditional inner-city bus or rail line. Two crew members are required to operate each Vaporetto: a driver and a doorman of sorts, who loops a rope around a post at each stop and opens the gate to direct passengers on or off the boat. I tried to imagine living in Venezia and using the Vaporetti system to commute to work, but existing without a car (or even a driveway!) is beyond me. Maybe if I stayed here for a month or two and adapted to a wheelless existence, I'd be able to envision everyday life on the Venetian islands. Today I felt very much a tourist, marveling at every turn, my camera in my outstretched hand continuously snapping photos. I must have resembled a limber Statue of Liberty, holding a camera aloft instead of a torch and clutching my purse in my other hand.

We watched as people hopped on and off at every stop and chose their seats or their square of floor until the taxi arrived at Piazza San Marco, where we debarked and headed to the Doge's Palace. There were no lines today but the Secret Itinerary was sold out so we weren't able to experience the entire sight. I'd been reluctant to buy tickets to sights before our trip, unwilling to adhere to a strict schedule on such a long trip; I was learning already this was an unwise choice, and I probably should have had one scheduled day at each city rather than allowing long lines or smarter tourists to dictate our itinerary.

The Doge's Palace, or at least the part we were allowed to see, is grand. It took an unfathomable eight hundred years to build and houses the governor's living quarters as well as all of the political offices, governmental meeting spaces, courts and prison. The paintings and mosaic artwork are awe-inspiring, and the sheer scale of each room increases the grandeur.

We wandered along with other travelers to stand

in salons and courtrooms, then proceeded to the prison to witness tiny stone cells. The last place on earth many prisoners ever saw, the Bridge of Sighs, was under construction so we were only allowed to enter part of it and see a view somewhat obstructed by the tarpaulins covering the scaffolding, a tiny window allowing light in. We left the ghosts to their sorrowful business and greeted the sunshine in the center courtyard, a welcome change from the depressing prison tour.

San Marco's bell tower already boasted a line of at least two hundred people snaking along the edge of the square. We located a lunch bar and ordered two sandwiches and a *caffe Americano* (an American coffee, which is really just hot water added to Espresso) and perched on the edge of a bench in the sun in the northeastern corner of the piazza along with 50,000 other people. Steph bought a zip-up sweatshirt from a street vendor to wear for our day's adventure. White with a pink ITALIA blazing across the chest, she bought it for €20 after negotiating down from €25. The quality didn't look worthy of $30, but we reminded each other we were competing with several thousand tourists, plenty of whom were willing to pay top dollar for Italian mementos. She posed with a few Venetian masks but didn't end up purchasing any.

We chose a Vaporetto heading toward the fish tail of the city and hopped off briefly to walk through a park. These were the first trees and grass we'd seen since arriving in Venezia, and although the morning was slightly chilly and a bit damp, we walked down a few botanical paths to visit nature for a few minutes. After capturing digital proof of Venetian trees we meandered down the seaside walkway for a while before returning to catch another Vaporetto, this time bound for San Michele, or Cemetery Island.

San Michele proved to be fairly far from the Venetian shores and the Vaporetto we'd chosen took the long way, through the city, past the canalside restaurants and palaces, past the cruise ship approaching town, through the back 'alley' featuring squat brick buildings painted with corporate logos: McDonald's, Adidas, Toyota.

Steph wore long (by American standards) shorts that ended just above her knees and earned several derogatory stares and snorts, and continued to hear wolf whistles and "*ciao, bella*" called out in suggestive tones. I'd taken to glaring at some of the men but they were undeterred by my evil eyes.

"They have meat-eating eyes," said Steph. She looked piqued, weary of public notice.

We finally arrived at San Michele and debarked along with most of the other passengers, this particular Vaporetto stopping at only one other island before returning to the city. I'd read a bit about San Michele before our trip, and the part I remembered most was the real estate challenge faced by trying to inter so many thousands of people in such a strictly confined area. One of the solutions to people seeking this highly exclusive resting place for their remains is to offer it for a certain number of years, then relocate the remains to another cemetery on the mainland. How unrestful!

We wandered between the gravestones, reading a few of the inscriptions on the more ornate ones and peering into the familial crypts circling each section of the cemetery. Energetic lizards provided light entertainment as they scuttled from warm granite slab to warm granite slab, disappearing before we could capture them on film.

Leaving San Michele we decided to debark the Vaporetto on the east side of Venezia and explore another *sestiare* (section or district of the city) on the way back to our hotel. This neighborhood was filled with shops, people and street entertainers and before we knew it we were facing the Rialto bridge, a mere few hundred feet from our hotel door. We sought out the Frari church, listed in Rick Steves' book as a two-star attraction, and ate dinner at a small café on Frari square.

The waitress at the café appeared annoyed, standing in the doorway wearing cowboy boots and a skirt, her face screwed into a scowl as we requested a seat inside. We'd spent the day outside and we were ready to escape the wind for a little while. She seated us in the back corner next to a cooler with a glass door and presented us with menus. The cooler was turned sideways, positioned so we couldn't see its contents from our seats.

After we placed our orders I gazed around the café and realized there wasn't a visible kitchen, or even a doorway to one, anywhere. Another worker was perched behind the bar, which offered a few stools and had an impressive display of wine and liquor along the back wall shelves. The waitress carried a dishpan to the cooler, opened the door and selected two items. She carried these in the dishpan high above her head to the other side of the bar, where she bent down to work. I turned in my chair and craned around to look inside the cooler to confirm my suspicions: we were eating TV dinners.

"She is nuking our food," I whispered to Steph.

"What?"

"This cooler. It's not a cooler, it's a freezer. They keep the meals in there and stick them in the microwave." Several beeps punctuated my words.

"Oh my god, we should warn the people next to us," Steph nodded toward the next table, two people still contemplating which 'gourmet' entrée to order. By this time, after walking and riding the Vaporetto all day, we were too hungry to bother finding another place to dine. We chose to stay and eat the nuked offerings, but when the waitress delivered my gelatinous asparagus risotto and Steph's congealing cheese ravioli we gagged on the first few bites.

That evening, our last in Venezia, I reviewed our

itinerary and realized Mestre is a nearby city and not the name of the train station in Venezia as I'd thought. We would have to catch an earlier Vaporetto than we'd planned, debark at the Venetian train station and catch a train to Mestre. There we would find our train to Firenze.

The first leg of our trip had passed quickly and we were both a little sad to leave Venezia, although we felt we'd seen everything we wanted to see. Venezia's carnival atmosphere is tiring and reminds one of a grand performance where the shopkeepers and waiters are all actors on a stage, presenting their best faces for the audience. We'd both noticed the threadbare seat cushions, unraveling table cloths and frayed uniforms, suggesting the state of 'elegant decay' extends to the people as well as the city itself.

Front door to our hotel

Chapter Three
Traveling from Venezia to Firenze and Siena
martedi (Tuesday)

Ti sta a pennelo.
It fits you like a paintbrush.
(It looks like it was made for you.)

The following morning we woke early, ate quickly and wished Jacqueline a happy day before catching the Vaporetto to the Venetian train station. Stephanie left Jacqueline a note where she'd find it when she cleaned our room, thanking her for everything and letting her know we enjoyed our stay.

We'd only spoken to Dani for a few minutes since she left for Alaska and this morning, we both wished she were with us to witness Venezia's sunrise.

Daylight broke as we floated up the Grand Canal one last time, silently bidding farewell to

Venezia and its magic. The city was just waking up, stretching and preparing for the day as deliverymen piloted their loaded boats and hand-trucked cases of soda and water to stores and restaurants.

The Vaporetto deposited us at the bottom of a flight of stairs, which we struggled up carrying our backpacks and large carry-on bags, to behold the muted chaos of the early morning train station. People rushed about, confidently navigating from door to ticket window to train, pausing to validate their tickets by inserting one end into one of several red machines scattered along the end of the platforms. We bought our tickets to Mestre then stood in the middle of the lobby, rocks amidst the ever-moving stream of people, until a businessman approached us to ask in English if we needed help. I showed him our tickets and he deftly pointed to the proper train and reminded us to stamp our tickets before boarding.

The Mestre train station proved a tiny bit easier to navigate due to our recent lesson in Venezia. After grabbing a quick breakfast, we quickly located a validation machine and stamped our tickets before boarding our train. We had reserved seats from here to Firenze, so we stowed our bags and settled in, each of us next to a window and facing each other with a table between us. Like typical Type As, we were seated a full twenty minutes prior to departure. Our seat mates arrived momentarily and likewise stowed their luggage in the overhead bins and between the backs of the seats. Clumsy introductions revealed a wide language barrier, but everyone seemed cheerful enough. Steph's neighbor was a portly young girl, seams straining and flesh spilling into Steph's seat. She had to raise the arm rest between them to accommodate her girth. As she was wedging herself into the space a petite, sixtyish nun in full habit with a knee length skirt busily arranged her luggage and raided her purse for tissues before settling in the seat next to me. The nun's head cold required frequent nose-blowing, and every five or six minutes throughout the trip she reached across me to deposit her tissues in the garbage container on the wall below the window. Unfortunately the container itself was missing—only the top of it was in place—so each tissue fell straight to the floor. The table between our seats apparently blocked the nun's view of the rapidly growing pile of detritus. Steph caught my eye and we chuckled every time the nun opened the lid and tossed her trash on my feet.

The scenery changed from terra cotta rooftops and blooming trees to mountains, flat farmland and rolling hills. Vineyards with staked grapevines in meticulous grid patterns, tunnels and limestone flashed by our windows. I'm no geologist but I recognize limestone, as it's prevalent in our end of the UP. We were gliding through the Dolomites.

The train finally halted and we hurriedly grabbed our unwieldy backpacks from the overhead compartments and wedged our way down the aisle toward the door, only to be forced back as far as the first empty seat to allow an enormous woman, wider than the train aisle, to ooze past us. She had to walk strategically so her hips popped into the space in front of each seat as she stepped, claiming the right-of-way with her massive girth.

We had the same train station situation here as in Venezia—we arrived at a station on the outskirts of Firenze, Rifredi, and had to catch a short train to the center of the city, Santa Maria Novella station. SMN was as I'd pictured it from my research. Steph and I located the *baggalio deposito* (baggage deposit) and checked our backpacks for €13,80 and wandered around waiting for Siw.

Siw (pronounced 'Seeve' like Steve without a 't') was our Norwegian exchange student in 1985-1986. She and I maintained sporadic contact but hadn't seen each other in twenty-four years. When I emailed Siw to tell her I would be on her continent, she arranged to join us for a few days along with her daughter. We had planned to meet Siw and Susanne (pronounced Soo-*sah*-na) at the train station on the outside stairs, but they were late. Steph and I sat on the top step so we could observe taxis and buses arriving as well as people walking back and forth; no Siw. The electric trains, mopeds, cars and natural gas buses whizzed by on the street below, feeding our impatience. The focus of Firenze is frenetic movement—rather shocking after languid Venezia.

We inspected each taxi that entered the train station, thinking Siw had called a cab from the airport. After waiting an additional fifteen minutes I called her and discovered she'd been unable to call me from her cell phone, and was waiting for us on the stairs around the corner (there are two sets of stairs; we'd each thought we were waiting on the only set). We met inside the train station at the tabacchi shop, easily finding each other.

After greeting Siw and Susanne and introducing our daughters, we helped them check their bags and struck out toward the Ponte Vecchio, the famous jewelry-store-lined bridge spanning the Arno River. Until now, I'd known the Arno River only as an obscure crossword puzzle answer.

Siw's voice sounded the same and I would have recognized her anywhere, her trim, petite frame and blonde pixie cut. I'd forgotten about her sarcastic wit but quickly adapted as we resumed our insult exchange ritual we'd begun in 1986. Our meeting in Italy as forty-year-olds, unlikely as the scenario would have seemed in '86 had we conceived the notion back then, felt normal, expected and comfortable as we slipped into our roles as pseudo-sisters and genuine friends. We bantered effortlessly, planning our days together after weighing every option and rejecting the least feasible or interesting ones.

"What the heck happened to your finger, there?" asked Siw, spying the grayish-green skin.

"Oh, I have some kind of skin problem, eczema or something, and it broke out just before we left home. It looks worse than it feels."

"Take it to the Farmacia—they can fix everything here. You don't need a doctor."

"Like a pharmacy?"

"Yeah—there's one across the street." We crossed and entered the Farmacia, walking to the back of the store where the pharmacist was bent over counting pills.

"*Ciao*," he greeted us.

"*Ciao. Parla inglese?*" I asked if he spoke English.

"*Si.*"

"I need something for this…" I showed him the finger in all its ominous green glory.

He inhaled sharply. "Oh. This is bad but I can fix. You need antibiotic," I nodded in agreement. "You need antibacterial," I nodded again, "and you need pain medication."

"Yes! *Si!* Do you have something for this?"

He reached behind him to select a tube of cream and presented it to me. "This is €14,90. Use it two times each day until all color is restored."

I shoved my money across the counter. "*Grazie.*"

We left the Farmacia for the madness of the street. Chattering above the city's roar, we wove through throngs of people walking and bicycling, occasionally moving aside to allow a tiny car to pass by. The scene was one of mildly organized chaos as thousands of tourists with no clear destination mingled with commuters and locals.

An elegantly dressed woman calmly cycled through the melee, her pumps hooked around the pedals and her hat floating above the crowd. She carried a purse on her forearm and wore a skirt and long dress coat. Her back was so straight she probably could have balanced a stack of books on her head without a wobble. Crowds parted and traffic paused as she pedaled confidently down sidewalks and across streets.

After visiting the bridge we paused for a snack and shopped our way back to the train station to retrieve our bags. By now Steph and I were using our limited Italian shopping comments as if we'd been born talking this way: *ciao* or *buon giorno* upon entering a store; *quanto costa* while holding up a garment to inquire about the price; *grazie* and another *ciao* upon exit. Immersion in the Italian language was similar to a real-life word puzzle, presenting easy-to-difficult challenges like the different days of the week in the New York Times crosswords. *Farmacia* (pharmacy); *hospitale* (hospital); *pomodoro* (tomato); *fragola* (strawberry); *scarpe* (shoes); *pantaloni* (pants). And my favorite: *sconte* (discount)! Just walking down the street reading the traffic signs, movie posters and store window displays helped me expand my Italian vocabulary. Eavesdropping on other shoppers and diners improved my pronunciation and increased my understanding of how the words fit together.

Siw and I found the bus station across the street from the train station just as the Rick Steves guide book promised, and used the hour-plus bus ride to catch up on the past twenty-four years and get to know each other's daughters. Dusk arrived and rain clouds rolled in as the bus left Firenze so most of the scenery passed by unwitnessed. We sat in the back seat and listened to the rain, trying to imagine the view judging by the ups and downs and sweeping curves all the way to Siena, where the rain let up as we emerged from the bus to a freshly rinsed city aglow with street lights.

Our hotel was around the corner from the bus station and we found it easily. The Albergo Bernini features a rustic front door with stairs leading up to a vintage reception desk complete with slots on the wall to hold the room keys, each one attached to a pool ball with the corresponding room number on it. The keys (large skeleton keys) are meant to be left at the front desk when one leaves the hotel during the day (we didn't realize this right away and carried the huge keychain around for part of one day).

The room Steph and I chose had a double bed and a single bed, a nice in-room bathroom with very little water pressure and a spectacular view from the large window near the double bed. There were no phones in the rooms but the common room had one guests could use with a calling card, and the rooftop terrace looked inviting and offered an even better view of the city. All windows were shuttered and screenless just like the ones in Venice, shedding generous natural light on the intricate geographic patterns on the linoleum floors. Siw and Susanne were situated down the hall in a similar room, but theirs featured a limited view of the street.

After quickly unloading and settling into our rooms we set out in search of dinner, which we found two blocks away in a second-story pizzeria with a waiter who spoke impeccable English. His language ability was both comforting and disappointing, removing my obligation to assault his ears with my pidgin Italian.

The day caught up to us immediately after dinner and we staggered back to the hotel to sleep. Siena felt comfortable and I was glad I'd chosen this city over frantic, frenzied Firenze to stay for four days. We heard very little traffic and no high heels tip-tapping past our windows and slept soundly with the window cracked open. We'd traveled by boat, train, bus and foot today, a total of 325 kilometers or 202 miles, not counting all of the shopping in Firenze.

Siena, for all its size and slight case of sprawl, tucks in early and sleeps soundly, its little village heart barely maintaining a quiet rhythm until morning when it wakes up with the sun and gently greets the day.

Siena, veiwed from the Albergo Bernini

Chapter Five
Siena
mercoledi (Wednesday)

Per me, solo un ditto di vino.
For me, only a finger of wine.
(For me, a splash of wine.)

The next day dawned clear and breezy. It's probably breezy every day in Siena, situated as it is atop a knobby hill, and I lamented my backpack contents once again: two pairs of Capris but only one sweater. The Capris wouldn't see the light of day on this trip until we reached the Amalfi coast, and even then for only one measly afternoon. The sweater, however, became my uniform. I wore it over every shirt I'd packed.

Market Day in Siena occurs every Wednesday (*mercoledi*) and seems to be where the locals buy everything from fruit and meat to clothing, plants and housewares. When I discovered Siena's weekly shopping extravaganza in my research it sounded so fun I built the first week's schedule around it, knowing all four of us would enjoy browsing through the street market booths.

The morning was cold, just this side of bitter, as we walked up the hill to the market area. It was set up at the bus station and commandeered an area the size of two or three city blocks, winding around the building and down the street, ascending a flight of stairs at the far end. Most of the booths featured tarp or tent walls and ceilings and many had a van at the back of the shopping area to use as a fitting room. Steph started bargain hunting right away and wore me out quickly as she found new clothes in every other booth.

We lost Siw and Susanne several times in the throngs of people packed wall to wall along the aisles between booths as we browsed and bartered. Steph and Susanne purchased a large enough wardrobe to hold a fashion show later that evening in the hotel while Siw and I sipped white wine and provided commentary (she won't drink red; I'm not so picky).

After exhausting ourselves at the market we left our purchases at the hotel and continued to Siena's famous square, Il Campo, to eat lunch at an outside restaurant in the sun across from the bell tower. Steph had been pining for a smoothie and I noticed an entry on the menu—*centrifughe frutta*—and recognized the first word as something close to 'centrifuge'. We'd found a smoothie! She ordered a kiwi pear *centrifughe* and pronounced it the best one she's ever had.

Siw and Susanne nattered in Norwegian, laughing and then explaining to us what they'd been discussing. Susanne studies English in school and possesses a large vocabulary but is not yet comfortable communicating in English when she wants to say something quickly. I grabbed my camera to take a photo of the famous square while we waited for our food.

Susanne held out her hand. "I'll take your picture," she offered. I handed her the camera and leaned toward Steph. "Smee-lay," Susanne sang out.

"Smee-lay? Is that smile?" I asked.

"Oh. Yes, it is Norwegian for smile," she demonstrated a shy smile.

"Smee-lay," Steph and I sang out, grinning for the camera.

Lunch re-energized us and we set out to explore the shopping avenue that extends from Il Campo uphill toward our hotel. Steph entered every hair salon we passed to inquire about the price of highlights and a cut (€110 - €120, equivalent to $165 - $180) but she wasn't prepared to pay that much yet. In the UP we usually pay around $30 for the same service, offered with a side of gossip in our own language.

Siena's stores offer many interesting items from

"San Jimmeen-yanno," I replied.

"Let's just call it San Jimmy. It's easier and it'll save time," said Siw. I agreed.

My finger, after one day of treatment, was nearly healed. The miracle cream would end up in our bathroom cabinet at home, to be doled out prudently over the next several months of various skin conditions. It's not available in the States without a prescription because it contains steroids and, in my doctor's opinion, is more powerful than necessary. This appeals to me after experiencing the rapid healing of my nearly rotted finger!

Scrivera, the Italian word for write, evokes an artful blend of 'scribe' and 'scribble'. It is so much more interesting and descriptive than our pedestrian English version, I feel like I'm doing something more active than writing a book if I am *scrivere un libro* (remember to roll the Rs!). I keep my moleskine notebook in my purse and jot (hopefully unobtrusively) in restaurants, on benches and buses, and every evening I summarize the day, reliving the details and studying our experiences.

Every expenditure is listed at the end of the book, so if one cover is opened a diary is revealed but if the book is flipped around and the other cover pried up a daily expense record is there to fill in any missing information.

Odd thoughts and random lists are entered as they're conceived. Today's entry includes a list of observations about Siena:

    Steep, narrow (but walkable) streets
    Respectful drivers, careful pedestrians
    Distinctively patterned cobblestones
    Friendly shopkeepers
    Beautiful architecture
    Tall stone buildings
    Delicious food
    Busy without being frantic
    Energetic and invigorating rather than exhausting
    Interestingly twisty streets
    Comfortable, clean city

I could scribble all day until the list grows as long as Siena's main shopping avenue. *Scrivera.*

The ubiquitous Smart Car

Chapter Eight
Siena
giovedì (Thursday)

Lui guida una vecchia caffettiera.
He's driving an old coffeepot.
(He's driving a jalopy.)

Armed with Daniela's map and instructions, we set out the next morning in search of the car rental company. Our map was not to scale and didn't contain every street—one would think I'd adapted to the substandard maps and learned to allow for these inaccuracies by this stage of the trip, but for some reason I continued to rely solely on the printed map. This resulted in a circuitous route around the Palio, which is the famed horse racing arena near downtown Siena. As we walked around its high walls, unable to see the interior, I realized I'd missed a turn one block back and lengthened our morning walk. We walked around three sides of the stadium, pretending to enjoy the scenery. All we could see was the tall brick wall on our right and a city street on our left.

"How are you doing with your map there?" asked Siw.

"Great! I was just going to tell you, this is the famous horse racing arena. This is actually a sight to see. People come from all over to watch the horse races here every year."

"Yah, it's fascinating. Quite the sight," Siw's eyes glinted with mischief, her sarcastic delivery pitch perfect and enhanced by her accent. "These are beautiful bricks, all stacked up so straight and tall. Good tourist sight."

I scrambled for another reason to justify my poor map translation. "It's so chilly this morning, it's good for us to walk an extra few feet so we can warm up. It's all part of my fitness program. Now we'll be able to eat pasta for lunch without worrying."

"Oh, great. I was awake all night worrying about eating pasta for lunch." The girls were trailing behind us, too sleepy to complain about the long walk.

"I can see my breath, Mom," was Steph's only comment.

Eventually we found the car rental place, which was half a block from an intersection indicated on the map as a standard four-square street crossing, but was in fact an offset intersection of only two streets with one curving around and creating another 90 degree corner a half block from its meeting with the other street. The door was locked, a handwritten sign on the glass urging us to go around the corner to the auto repair shop.

"This entire trip is like a scavenger hunt," I said.

We turned in the direction the arrow indicated and found a hair salon. Steph ran inside to check on the prices and met Paolo, a hairdresser who speaks English, and his staff of Italian-language-only girls. Every time we take a vacation, Steph wants to have her hair cut and colored, but logistics usually don't allow for it. This hair salon, *Coiffeur Donnini*, charged a fair price (compared to the other overpriced salons she'd checked earlier) and Paolo was friendly and accommodating, grinning after every awkward sentence. After extensive explanations dutifully repeated back from Paolo to ensure he understood exactly what she wanted, she made an appointment for the next morning.

The car rental place occupied a two-story building and was constructed entirely of poured concrete. We entered at the street-level top story to sign papers and agree on the terms, then trundled downstairs to the alley-level basement floor (-1 *piano*) and out the back door to inspect the car.

"This car, it's automatic," explained the rental agent, sweeping her hands toward it like Vanna White revealing a puzzle. She circled the vehicle pointing out various dings, dents and scratches, while Siw took a photo of each blemish. We piled into the car—a two-door requiring a shoehorn to enter the back seat—and drove out of the crooked little alley, finding ourselves next to the city wall. The car rental place is built on both sides of the massive brick wall, possibly designed to offer a secret escape in medieval days.

After driving a few blocks we realized the 'automatic' car has an automatic clutch but requires manual shifting—there was a plus sign and a minus sign, above and below the shifter, and Siw had to let up on the gas and nudge the shifter forward to shift to the next highest gear. Siena, city of curly streets and substandard maps, kindly ejected us in the right direction just as I convinced myself we'd missed our turn.

Italian highways are decorated with signs indicating the next town with an arrow to reassure drivers they're on the correct road (rather than sporting signs revealing the actual name of the highway one is traveling, like in the good old US of A). Viewing a map of Tuscany, or Toscana, the first thing I noticed was the silly-string (or maybe spaghetti?) configuration of highways, some of them looping about so madly they nearly cross themselves. It's virtually impossible to tell which compass direction one is facing; as soon as I figured it out, we'd take another hairpin corner, all of us sliding to one side of the car (Siw wasn't too heavy on the brake, relying on willpower to keep us on the road).

We could see San Gimignano from several vantage points along the route, perched atop a large hill, majestic and beckoning. The parking lot just outside the city walls proved easy to navigate and we exited the car, rushing toward the gate. The main street of San Jimmy is lined with stores and extends in a fairly straight line from the gate to the town square.

In the UP, form follows function when it comes to fashion. We wear scarves for four to six months of each year, not as a fashion accessory but as a health necessity to help prevent a chill and aid in breathing when the air temperature dips so low it's all but impossible to inhale without filtering the incoming air through a scarf to heat it up before breathing it in. The concept of a fashionable scarf is something we expect to see in magazines or on television, but who would bother wearing a scarf just for looks? One made from Grandma's wool scraps is more effective than some cashmere snippet. Each year, by the time spring thaws the ground sufficiently to render winter jackets unnecessary, we're only too eager to jettison the scarves we've been diligently stowing in the arms of our coats all winter long, wrapping around our necks and mouths. We're ready to expose some skin to the sun (but not too much; it's not as if frostbite is completely unheard of in June!).

Many of San Gimignano's stores, like those in Venice and Florence, lure shoppers with their colorful scarves, draped silk or cashmere strips to create artful displays that collectively contain a force so powerful even a function-only scarf wearer like myself reaches for my wallet to dole out Euros, buying several colors of the nearly-useless strips thick enough to keep me warm only in May or September. Of course, they don't go with my spring jacket or fall jacket; I'll need another of each.

Another San Jimmy favorite is the wild boar, *il porcino*, (ill pore-*chee*-noh) prominently featured in many store display windows and on restaurant menus. Susanne looked horrified when she first spied a wild boar, poised in a shop window as if preparing to attack an innocent shopper.

"Would you like a wild boar for a pet?" I asked Susanne.

"Nnooo," her eyes were round.

"Maybe you could try eating one for lunch. It looks like they make lots of different sausages from *il porcino*."

She shook her head with a grimace. "No, I won't like that," she shivered.

One store was impossible to pass by, its entryway featuring leather purses, bags, satchels and totes. By this time my purse search was beginning to annoy everyone, including myself, and I knew I had to kill the obsession with a purchase. As usual, I entered the store and inhaled sharply, filling my lungs with the rich, luxuriant scent of fresh leather. It's enough to make one dizzy with leather lust. I briefly considered purchasing every item in the store just so I could cram it all in my closet and maintain my own leather-scented retreat. Once I acclimated to the scent and my senses returned, I found two purses I liked and decided to visit the same store on the way back out of town.

After escaping the leather store we browsed at a street market established in the town center, then sought lunch in a small restaurant just across the square from the bell tower. The restaurant was a nondescript café offering deli-style sandwiches for fairly cheap prices. We ate and paid our bills, then Steph and I wandered to the back of the building to find the ladies' room. Upon exiting the ladies' room, a frail dowager started yelling and pointing her finger at us. I listened closely until I recognized the phrase '*solo cliente en banyo*', which I interpreted to mean 'only customers in the bathroom'.

"*Mi dispiace,*" I apologized, pointing at myself and Steph. "*Cliente, si, si. Mi dispiace.*" I made frantic eating gestures, then paying gestures, pointing continually at both of us and repeating my apology until she calmed down. Finally she grinned at us, revealing a few gray teeth, and waved a nearly translucent hand in the air.

"*Cliente*, ok, ok," she said. "*Buon giorno. Mi dispiace. Giorno.*" We left her there, perched on the edge of her chair, skeletal legs crossed and slumped over so her ribs made ridges in the back of her shirt.

"Where were you guys?" asked Siw as we jogged out of the restaurant. "We're ready to go up in the bell tower. This is the view you've been waiting to see," she gestured with her hand. "Or is this one not in your tour book?" Siw constantly teased me about my tour book, pointing out how non-spontaneous my travel habits were, but she always referred to the book when we needed information.

"Oh, don't worry, it's in the Rick Steves. He's going to accompany us up the steps of the San Jimmy bell tower. We were just chatting with an old woman about using the bathroom."

"Yeah, it's a good thing Mom knew what she was saying. That lady was angry!" said Steph.

"If she'd talked a little slower it wouldn't have taken me so long to figure out what she was saying, but it all worked out in the end."

We entered the bell tower, checked our belongings at the bottom and started climbing stairs. The stairs are all metal, ascending up the interior of the tower, terrifyingly skinny open grates with a breathtaking view all the way to the bottom, but as long as I focused forward or upward my knees didn't shake. Steph made it nearly to the top—she was on the last flight, which isn't a stairway but a narrow ladder made of the same metal grating with pipe railings, and had to back down. She just couldn't envision a way to step from the ladder to the platform at the top, so she backed down and started working her way down the stairs while we emerged at the top and enjoyed the views for a few minutes. The vista stretched from the town directly below us and the other nearby towers to beautiful Tuscan farms and vineyards, rolling verdant hills punctuated by trees and segmented by twisting roads.

For a moment, I forgot we still had to climb back down.

The descent proved difficult, as I couldn't look forward without risking missing a step (I'm notorious for tripping on a perfectly smooth surface and once broke my tailbone walking down the stairs in my own house). I had to watch my feet and plan each step, but after the first half-flight the grates became an optical illusion, the ones supporting me blending with the ones three flights down and two flights below those. My breath was caught in my throat, my knuckles white from gripping the railing (both hands on the same railing so I crept downward half-twisted toward the banister). Those ascending, blithely climbing while focusing upward and forward, granted me a wide berth. Some of them commented on acrophobia, applauding my courage and grim determination. At least, I think that's what they were saying. The rushing sound in my ears prevented all sounds except my ominously thundering heartbeat from penetrating my consciousness.

I nearly kissed the ground when I reached it, not because I was so relieved, which I was, but because after the strain of traversing several hundred stairs in a near-crouching posture my knees nearly buckled when I stood up straight.

After surviving the San Gimignano bell tower we shopped our way back to the car, pausing to purchase the purses I'd found earlier (one for me, one for my sister) and cramming our bags into the back seat with the girls. We set out once again, Siw driving while I navigated, in search of Volterra. The road looped and twisted, nearly turning back on itself until I wondered aloud whether we were indeed on the correct road. We hadn't yet seen a sign indicating we were traveling in the direction of Volterra and we both started to worry we were on the wrong path. The rental car had to be returned by 6:00 pm to avoid late fees, so time was an important consideration.

We careened around a generous curve and saw a tour bus with a large sign on it reading "San Gimignano". Siw stopped in the middle of the road and I jogged over to the tour guide. Before I could ask if she spoke English, she greeted me.

"You lost?" she grinned.

"Well, we're looking for Volterra and just wondered if we're on the right road. We just came from San Gimignano." I explained.

"Yes, continue on this road and watch the signs at the roundabout. You'll like Volterra—it's a pretty cool little town," she smiled again and turned toward her group.

"*Grazie*! Thank you! *Buon giorno*," I called to her as she waved me on.

Rick Steves calls Volterra "…real, vibrant, and almost oblivious to the allure of the tourist dollar. A refreshing break from its more commercial neighbors, it's my favorite small town in Tuscany." By the time we entered the parking garage the mist was gathering strength, growing from mini-drops to real raindrops, so we walked quickly through the ancient city wall to stroll along the narrow streets. My tour book was collecting raindrops, puckering its pages, and Steph kept reminding me to put it away.

Volterra features interesting, life-like ceramic pieces in most of its shops, colorful displays of realistic-looking vegetables and fruits beckoning one inside. I wanted to purchase a bowl full of ceramic grapes and lemons, but wondered how I'd carry them home and what I'd do with them once I did. I could almost hear my husband's derisive comment about "dust-collectors". I silently agreed with him and passed the exquisite pieces, only to be confronted with them again and again in every store.

We eventually stumbled upon the Archeological Park, along the southern edge of town, and quickly lost our sense of direction. I was sure we could exit on the side of the parking garage, neatly looping back to our car, but this was apparently not the case. Two municipal workers were shoveling dirt into a wheelbarrow, so I approached them for help.

"*Mi scusi, parla inglese?*" I asked. Excuse me, do you speak English?

One guy turned and responded, "*Si, paco.*" Yes, a little.

"*Dovè…*" I gestured at the parking garage on the map, asking 'where…'.

"Ah, you must first proceed back to the gate. When you reach the gate, it will be necessary to turn left." He waved his arm in the general direction of the gate, checking with me to make sure I was nodding in understanding.

"*Si, si,*" I said.

"At that particular time, it will be necessary to proceed down the road until you come upon the parking garage."

"*Si, grazie,*" I thanked him.

"*Prego, prego.*" You're welcome, you're welcome.

On our way back to Siena we passed a sign announcing a small town named Montereggioni. The sign had a castle-like border across the top, and up ahead we could see the turrets rising above the road.

"Want to stop there? We have time," asked Siw.

"Yeah, this is our chance to be spontaneous. This town isn't even in the book!" I told her. The girls groaned in the back seat. After our day of shopping in the cold rainy weather they were both ready to eat a hot meal and return to the hotel, but Siw and I were determined to experience something unscheduled.

We parked the car in the parking lot outside town and proceeded up the walkway to the castle wall, leaving Steph in the car to rest and read her book. Montereggioni is a teeny tiny town, probably 500 paces from one end to the other, with little market-style stalls set up along the town square and a cobbler's store at one end of town. They allow people to climb atop the castle walls to view the Tuscan countryside, but we'd had enough climbing for one day and were more interested in the town itself. We toured the weaving studio and found a shop hidden down a narrow, twisting walkway and another one in a basement with an empty suit of armor standing guard. The views of Tuscany through the castle arches are fantastic and make the town worthy of a stop.

After our castle-town tour we piled back into the rental car and drove to Siena, stumbling upon the car rental place quite on accident while seeking a gas station. We found a gas station and then found the car rental place again, proud of ourselves for our clearly superior navigational and driving abilities. An older man with a sour expression walked out of the building with my mom. We've been to Rome and Venice already."

"So have we! Well, Venice anyway. We're ending in Rome. I'm Jan and this is my daughter Stephanie. Our friends, Siw and Susanne, are from Norway so they just flew down to meet us for four days. Where are you going next?"

"Sorrento, then back to Rome."

"No way! That's where we're going." My eyebrows must have disappeared above my hairline, I was so shocked someone else had chosen a similar route. We compared schedules, and they nearly matched. Liam's mom Kate came out to check on him, her blue eyes sparkling and her smile matching her son's. We introduced everyone and made plans to join for lunch sometime during the remainder of our trip. I hoped our plans came to fruition, but I didn't really expect to see them again.

Firenzian door design

Chapter Thirteen
Firenze
venerdì (Friday)

Non fare il passo pici lungo della gamba.
Don't make your step longer than your leg.
(Don't bite off more than you can chew.)

We enjoyed breakfast the next morning with Kate and Liam, our new friends from Denver, who told us all about their adventures the day before. While we'd been tooling around Tuscany they had taken the bus to Pisa. We'd originally planned to visit the leaning tower but the bus and train schedules to Pisa made it impossible to make a quick trip and we were reluctant to sacrifice an entire day to one leaning tower. One tribulation of a major trip is the many compromises and decisions, choosing different sights over others, all without knowing which ones we would enjoy more,

George fame; the woman remained quiet, probably resigned to her husband's self-congratulatory commentary spiked with tight right views, his Archie Bunker personality in direct contradiction to his wild west-meets-Where's Waldo appearance.

I was asking Siw about the family trip she planned to take the next year, traveling to the US for a month. She has a niece living in Oregon, and we were discussing the distances around the lower 48 states and trying to figure out the best way to visit—either join her for a few days or have her come to our house so she could visit our whole family.

"It takes four to five hours to fly from Michigan to Oregon," I was thinking out loud.

"It's hard to believe how big your country is," she said.

"You should drive. You'll see more," interjected the Delaware-Texan.

"We drove to Florida once. It took 24 hours," said Steph.

"Florida sucks," said the Texan. "Nothin' but swamps and crocodiles and old folks livin' in trailer parks."

"Is Texas nicer?" I asked.

"I wouldn't know; I'm from Delaware," he drawled, cutting his eyes toward his wife. I wondered if he was in the Witness Protection program. If so, he needed more training.

"It's all the same, isn't it? The weather might be

different, but the culture is the same," said Siw.

"No, we have a different culture than down south, or California, or even the Eastern seaboard," I told her. "We have different food, fashion and climate than those places."

The Texan/Delawarese snorted, leaning forward. "You can't possibly think the inbred rednecks in Tennessee are anything like the fruits and nuts in California, the illiterate bastards from Louisiana or the shit kickers in Texas." He laughed. "And that's not even considering Indians, however many tribes there are, the ranchers in Montana, the hippies in the Pacific Northwest. Don't even get me started on immigrants, towelheads and 'people of color'," he made quotation marks with his long bony fingers in the air. "Hell, there must be 100 different cultures in the US of A. Obviously, some of them belong there and some of them don't." He barely moved when he spoke, his hat perched unmoving atop his head.

"We're from Michigan," said Steph.

"I know that. I can hear it in your accent," he said, his drawl suddenly more pronounced. As we gathered our stuff together I noticed his dinner plate belt buckle and wondered again why he insisted on pretending he was from Delaware. I felt sorry for his silent wife and considered the possibility of her silence being her way of balancing the loud and incessant delivery of his opinions and observations.

When we arrived in Firenze the first seller we encountered was an Asian man hawking rolling suitcases.

"*Quanto costa?*" I asked him, thinking we could easily stow our purchases on wheels and alleviate some of the weight from our backs for the remainder of our trip.

"Seventeen Euros," he responded.

Siw and I held a brief conference, deciding we needed three bags altogether. I turned back to the seller. "What if we buy three?" I asked him. At his puzzled look, I tried again, "*Quanto costa, tre?*" How much, three? I pointed at three different bags.

"*Si, si.* You can buy three bags." He held up his thumb and two fingers.

"*Trenta* Euros, *tre* bags?" I asked in a horrible mutation of English and Italian, thirty Euros for three bags.

"*Si, no. Quindici* each bag if you buy three." Fifteen Euros per bag for three bags.

"*Dodici?*" Twelve? Now I was just having fun practicing my numbers. He held a whispered debate with his partner, then came back to the table.

"*Tredici.* Okay. That's it, *si, si.*" Thirteen Euros. Final offer.

"Okay, we will return today and buy three bags."

He looked confused, but smiled and waved us on.

Our day in Firenze was uneventful, mainly spent shopping the markets and wandering the streets, people-watching and talking with Siw and Susanne. They were speaking Norwegian less often now that we'd been together for a few days and we were feeling more like a cohesive group than two pairs. We frequently separated when we encountered a market, our unspoken agreement being to stay within the group of stalls until we gathered together again before proceeding beyond the neighborhood. I found Steph, Siw and Susanne crowded around a jeweler's display, watching intently while he created a necklace for each of them from wire, bent into the shape of their names. His sign claimed he could make any name out of wire within three minutes for eight Euros, but the entertainment was free as he deftly formed the metal with perfect cursive swirls, his bushy eyebrows indicating deep concentration.

The rain made periodic appearances between intervals of sunshine, usually heralded by the choreographed appearance of hundreds of umbrellas before we realized it was misting. Street vendors selling sunglasses displayed on folding cardboard easels folded them up, stashed them behind a building and whipped out different folding cardboard easels, opening them to reveal umbrellas for sale. One had to watch closely but it was almost like seeing behind the curtain at the circus as they switched from one display to the next, then back again when the sun reappeared. I refused their offers of umbrellas, convinced it wouldn't add enough value to justify the cost. Another thing to carry held no appeal for me, my purse already heavy and full with my camera, the Rick Steves tour book, phrase book and maps of Firenze all jammed inside.

While the umbrellas didn't sway me, the leather did. I pined for a leather bookbag, a tote bag, satchel, and maybe three more purses. If we'd been closer to going home I would have spent several hundred Euros on leather goods, but since I'd have to carry my purchases for another week to two more cities and on countless trains I was reluctant to add to my luggage. Siw bought a leather jacket and wore it for the rest of the day.

Exhausted, we finally headed back to the bus station, pausing to purchase our previously agreed-upon wheeled bags, which already looked quite small considering the volume of our purchases. The seller first claimed to have no recollection of our earlier discussion, but I just kept repeating the deal and he finally nodded. Steph, Susanne and I chose our bags and stowed our purchases inside and continued toward the bus stop.

Once again we had our usual seats, the very last row across the back of the bus, and Liam found us. Kate relaxed in relative peace while Liam regaled us with wild tales, impressions of celebrities and promises to entertain us with card tricks and moonwalk demonstrations when we returned to the hotel. Liam was wearing his new sweatshirt, a royal blue hoodie with the word ITALIA emblazoned across the chest and a shield with Italy's colors, red white and green, on the upper left side.

"Is that like Italy's flag?" asked Siw.

"Yea, those are the colors. They just have three big stripes," Liam looked down at his shirt.

"It's not pretty like our flag. Ours is the best," said Steph.

"I've never seen a country as patriotic as yours," said Siw. "Do you still play the song every morning before school starts?"

"The national anthem? Of course. And we say the Pledge of Allegiance," answered Steph.

"Yeah, the Pledge. I remember saying that. In Norway we only hear our national anthem once a year, on Independence Day."

Steph and I laughed. "We hear the national anthem before every sporting event, Presidential speech and school function. It's even part of some rock and roll songs, country songs and nursery rhymes. It's everywhere. I can't imagine not seeing the flag or hearing the song; that must be so weird."

Liam said his school doesn't play the national anthem every morning but he does hear it at sporting events and other functions.

"Americans are the proudest ones," said Siw. "I

thought you guys would be walking down the street waving your flags when we met in Firenze the other day. That's why we couldn't find you—no flags waving!"

"I guess it's just part of our culture. We are proud as a country, and we're grateful for our freedom and our rights."

"Yeah, and even when you see another American, like that guy this morning at breakfast, you don't like him but you're both Americans so you stick together with your flags," Siw shook her head.

"Maybe other countries would display more flags if they were prettier," offered Steph. "No one wants to fly an ugly flag."

After a period of silence we asked Liam how he liked the museums and what he thought of Firenze. "It was fun. Pretty cool to see David. The only bad thing was Mom lost her camera."

"Oh no! She lost it in Firenze someplace?" Losing a camera halfway through vacation is unthinkable. It would be worse than breaking a bone while traveling.

"No, she first noticed it when we were on the bus this morning and she remembers setting it under the table in the common room so it's probably at the hotel. She's not too worried about it."

"Was it a big camera? I don't remember seeing anything on the floor, but I didn't set anything down there," I hoped they'd find the camera—Liam's photos of the leaning tower were on there.

"Yeah, it's a pretty big camera. I'm sure someone found it." I thought briefly of the Delaware-Texan, this morning his last at the hotel, and wondered if he was now lugging around a camera as large as his hat. "Mom bought it just for this trip—she said this trip deserved a big, expensive camera."

"She's right. I just have this little one because I didn't want to lug around a big one. I wish I brought a bigger one now that I'm here, though. I hope you don't lose your Pisa pictures."

"Those are the ones I'm worried about too. They're the only ones I want—if someone keeps the camera and just gives me those pictures I'd be happy."

By the time we exited the bus in Siena we were tired and hungry, so we decided to drop off our rolling suitcases and ask Daniela if there are any restaurants nearby. Susanne observed we hadn't eaten pizza yet, and since this was the last night the four of us would have together in Italy, we sought a pizzeria. Daniela knew of the perfect one, just around the corner from our hotel, that featured a spectacular view of Siena as well as a superb menu and wait staff. The evening was cool and we were reluctant to eat inside, not wanting to waste the view, so we sat near a propane column heater and wrapped our coats tighter. The pizza was fabulous, the city lit up like a post card. We ate hastily to avoid getting a chill and walked back around the corner to the Albergo Bernini.

Liam was waiting for us when we returned to the hotel, ready with his repertoire of tricks and demonstrations. Siw brought her tiny spherical speaker to the common room; we poured wine and enjoyed an eclectic blend of contemporary Norwegian and 1980s music. After applauding a couple of card tricks, Siw and Susanne offered to teach us a Norwegian card game called Idiot and we invited another guest who'd been on the phone throughout the card trick portion of the entertainment. She was traveling with her parents, celebrating her recent graduation from a University in Washington state and taking a break from her anthropological studies.

The game of Idiot, pronounced Id-yoot in Norwegian, relies on luck and chance and features random, convoluted rules. I won the game but I still have no idea how to play it. The entire game was punctuated with new rule announcements and suggestions from our Norwegian coaches. At one point, our laughter and cries of "Id-yoot!" reached a sufficient decibel to inspire the man across the hall to carry his alarm clock over and show us what time it was and share his early morning plans.

We all had early trains or buses to catch, so after the final round of Id-yoot we parted ways and retreated to our rooms. Kate and I had tentative plans to meet in Positano for lunch in a couple days, but we hadn't specified a restaurant or meeting place.

Kate had inquired with the hotel staff about her missing camera, but no one had turned it in. A thorough sweep of the common room revealed nothing, just as she'd expected. I mentioned the Delaware-Texan to Kate as a possible suspect, thinking the hotel might be willing to call and ask him if he'd seen the camera, but Kate just shook her head. "I'd rather not think about who might have taken it. It's gone and it's not like we'll get it back. I just wish they'd left the card with the photos of Venice and Pisa," she sighed. "Oh well, we still have our memories of Liam holding up the Leaning Tower."

Trenitalia

Chapter Twenty-One
Sorrento by Rail
sabato (Saturday)

L'asino chiama orecchia lung ail cavallo.
The donkey says the horse has long ears.
(The pot is calling the kettle black.)

We woke up early, dressing quickly in the pale light and allowing twenty minutes to say *buon giorno* to Siw and Susanne. Siw and I commented on future vacation plans, promising each other we wouldn't allow two dozen years to pass before meeting again. "If we do that, we are old ladies next time," she said with a grin.

"Smee-lay," I told Susanne. "Enjoy the rest of your vacation, and tell your English teacher all your new vocabulary words." Susanne smiled sadly and wished us well.

The taxi arrived ten minutes early, the driver leaping from the vehicle to grab our bags and toss them in the trunk. I was glad we were cruising the streets of Siena before most people were out of bed—since the city was built when life progressed at the speed of a clip clopping horse and all the buildings were constructed right to the edge of the streets, it's impossible to see if any traffic is approaching until entering the intersection. The driver's confidence helped mitigate my fear of a broadside collision and I sighed with relief when he stopped and announced our arrival at the train station.

"It's like a carnival ride. Who needs a Ferris wheel when you can just call a cab?" I said to Steph when I saw how large her eyes were.

We already had our tickets for this leg of the trip, so we walked up to the platform and set our bags down. Two shifty-looking men in their early twenties glowered at us, pacing around each other like two dogs while smoking cigarettes and flicking their ashes menacingly toward the tracks. I suddenly realized we'd forgotten to stamp our tickets in one of the validation machines sprinkled around the train station. Of course, there were no machines on the platform.

"You stay here and watch the bags," I told Steph. "I'll run as fast as I can and go stamp these."

"Don't leave me here with those creeps!" she whispered. The platform was starting to fill now, several other tourists and a few locals crowding around.

"You'll be okay. There are more people here now. I'll be right back. Just keep all the bags here and keep looking around so they know you're aware of them." I ran down the stairs, through the hallway and up the other set of stairs to the station, frantically searching for a ticket validating machine. I finally spied one near the door, nearly falling on my face as I approached it, my feet unable to keep up with my body's momentum. The tickets stamped and shoved back in my purse, I spun around and sprinted back down the stairs, through the hallway and up the stairs to the platform, sensing the possibility of an imminent cardiac event.

The train pulled up and we hopped on, settling into two bench seats facing each other, filling one with our bags to avoid sharing our space. The two hoodlums followed us and sat directly behind us, in seats on a raised platform two or three steps higher than ours. They situated themselves so they could look down on our heads.

Steph fell asleep, her head bobbing forward while I kept vigil and glared at the two hooligans. They spoke rapid Italian, their conversation punctuated with giggles after every few words. Their behavior made me increasingly uncomfortable. I listened intently to their speech, and when I was able to isolate a few words, my discomfort and anxiety ratcheted up. "*Bella carina,*" said one. Beautiful young girl. I thought of him as Tweedledee. "*Si, si, mama, figlia,*" replied Tweedledum, making smooching noises. Yes, yes, mother and daughter. I craned my head around until they met my eyes so they knew I'd heard and understood their comments. They gazed at me unabashed, so I slowly drew my finger across my throat in the universal gesture for "cut it out."

"*Basta,*" I muttered. Enough.

We had a layover and train change in Chiusi, so we hauled our packs and rolling bags inside in search of breakfast. The food was substandard and expensive, but we chose a small round table and ate. Tweedledum and Tweedledee paced around the station, gazing at us through half-open eyes as they sauntered past our table.

"I don't like them," said Steph. "They scare me."

"They're not going to try anything here," I told her, hoping I was right. "Hopefully they'll catch a different train than the one we're catching." I watched as Tweedledum hiked up his sagging pants, never dropping his gaze. It seemed as if he was deciding if he should rob us or rape us or both.

They suddenly trotted back out to the platform and boarded a train. I realized how tense I'd been since first encountering them that morning as my whole body suddenly felt lighter and less rigid. We still had an hour to wait and the crowded station seemed stifling now that we weren't worried about our personal safety.

We asked the guy behind the coffee counter about stowing our bags and he offered to do it for free, so we escaped the train station and ventured outside to downtown Chiusi, careful not to stray too far and miss our connecting train.

Entering an art and office supply store, I bought some sketching supplies for my daughter Dani and we learned the shopkeeper had travelled to the States several times and loved visiting our country. He'd explored New York City and the East Coast area. His store featured funky and unique stationery, pens, puzzles and gifts and I was happy to browse every nook.

I hoped the Italian sketch book and pencils would inspire Dani to sketch some Alaskan scenery; her latest painted canvas graced our dining room wall and I didn't want her to lose that talent.

We finally continued on our way, stopping in a gift store and two clothing stores as we worked our way back to the train station to retrieve our bags. We stamped our tickets and moved out to the platform as the train to Napoli arrived.

This train was clearly overbooked—we had specific seat assignments and many passengers stood in the aisle, which ran along one side of the train rather than down the center. Each seating section featured two benches facing each other, luggage racks overhead, and a little door to shut out the aisle commotion.

A fat, cheerful girl who spoke Spanish and wore mens' Spiderman underwear peeking jauntily above her sagging pants claimed a seat across from us until the first stop, when four new people boarded and evicted her from the seat. She kept giggling at us and asking Steph to watch her bag, offering us a view of Spidey every time she bent over.

Our seat mates debarked at the Roma Termini station, leaving us space to stretch out for the last and shortest leg of the ride to Napoli Centrale.

Viewing our picture book now, this day of travel is missing and creates a gap in the tale told through our camera lens. If it were possible to somehow rewind time and electronically record it, I would record our experience at Napoli Centrale, the large, chaotic, multi-level train station situated in a city hampered by its reputation and crime rate—a traveler's cautionary tale waiting to happen.

By the time the train stopped we were poised with our bags ready to leap out and find our next train, the Circumvesuviana, to Sorrento. We also had to buy tickets on the way to the train, since the inter-city train doesn't sell them online. I knew we had to go downstairs to board the next train but had no idea where to find the ticket window. We stood on the platform orienting ourselves, painstakingly translating the various signs. I didn't see any signs indicating the direction of the stairs or the other trains, but just as we were choosing a direction we heard an elderly porter bellowing, "Pompeii, Sorrento, Amalfi! Pompeii, Sorrento, Amalfi!" The urgency in his voice alerted us immediately.

"Maybe something changed or got cancelled," said Steph. "Should we ask him?"

"Yes," I rushed to the porter and said, "Sorrento Circumvesuviana."

"You have tickets?" he asked.

"No," we shook our heads.

He crooked his arm in a "follow me" gesture and strode quickly off the platform. As we entered the station, his pace quickened and he grabbed Steph's wheeled bag, rolling it along behind him. We glanced at each other, slightly alarmed, but he still seemed more helpful than harmful. We were walking at a manic pace, nearly jogging, and I reminded myself that even after sitting in the cramped quarters of the train and carrying fifty pounds on our backs, we shouldn't have so much difficulty keeping pace with a senior citizen.

I was walking abreast of the porter while Steph followed closely behind when I noticed his threadbare jacket had no name stitched on the chest. No company insignia was visible on his shirt, hat or jacket. There was no way for me to communicate this to Steph without his knowledge.

"This your first visit?" he asked.

I nodded. "*Sí.*"

"How long you stay?"

"Oh, a week or so," I glanced back at Steph and dropped back one step to walk next to her.

"Mom! I don't like him. Grab my bag!" she whispered.

"It's okay," I told her quietly. "I don't think he wants your bag. Just keep an eye out and don't let him lose us in the crowd."

The 'porter' effortlessly glided through the throngs of people, most of them obediently moving aside to allow us passage. Maybe it was his expression, determined and confident, or his 'uniform', quite realistic at first glance. Maybe it was simply his pace and the way he projected energy forward that caused people to vacate his path. Whatever it was, I knew we'd have never crossed the station so quickly even if we'd known where to go.

Suddenly we arrived at a ticket booth, several lines of people trailing toward each window. The porter stopped abruptly and said, "Money." He held out his hand.

"What?"

"Money. I get tickets for you. Come." He gestured to the front of the far right line, dragging

Steph's bag with him. I left my bag with her and followed him, opening my purse. The ATM in Chiusi hadn't worked and our funds had dwindled to €60, all of it together in one pocket. Feeling like a reckless gambler I gave a €10 note to him and he pushed the other bills back into my purse.

"Be careful," he stared at me. "Pickpockets here," he cautioned as he turned toward the ticket window.

By now Steph was nearing panic mode, hopping from one foot to the other. "Grab my bag!" She called out. The porter hadn't loosened his grip on the handle and I was unwilling to create an incident by wrestling with a seemingly helpful, geriatric man.

"Don't worry!" I called to Steph even as I wondered if this porter would abscond with my money or actually provide us with tickets.

"Here. Take." He thrust the tickets and money at me, which I crammed into my pocket so I wouldn't have to reopen my purse. The porter turned on his heel and approached the escalators, nodding at the attendant who greeted him and let us all through after viewing our tickets. The porter still gripped Steph's bag. I glanced at Steph to make sure she noticed the attendant had recognized our porter.

The escalator delivered us to the Circumvesuviana platform and Steph wrested her bag from the porter's fierce grasp.

"*Grazie*," I told him, attempting to wave him off.

"Wait here," he instructed, pointing at the cement. "First train no good. Second train you catch." He held up two fingers, then turned his hand over, palm up. "Tip." He pointed with his other hand at his open palm. "Ten," he demanded, "tip."

"Oh my god! He's ripping us off! Don't pay him," said Steph.

"I'll give him a tip. He saved us time—I wouldn't have run through the station that fast without getting lost." I dropped some coins in his hand.

"More," he pointed to his hand again, now filling with my coins.

"We don't even know if we're getting on the right train," Steph pointed out.

I gave her the tickets. "See if they say Sorrento," I said, digging in my pocket again and handing him some small coins.

"They say Sorrento," she confirmed.

"More," he demanded again.

"No, that's enough!" Steph said, grabbing his arm. "You need to go now. That's enough." She spoke with firm authority.

"We need this money to eat tonight," I explained. "It's all we have left." He turned slowly and slouched to the escalator, posing on his ascent like a reprimanded puppy.

"What a creep. Why did you give him money?" asked Steph. "I don't think he even works here. I thought he was going to help us until he grabbed my bag and starting sprinting through the train station." She was clearly shaken, as was I.

A family of three Americans were standing a few yards away, talking about Sorrento. I approached the mother and asked, "Are you catching the train to Sorrento?" They assured us we were in the right place. We shared our porter story and they commiserated, remarking how different the challenges are in a foreign country. They were from LA and traveled with three very large wheeled suitcases, each one large enough to stow the porter in, according to Steph.

The Californians traveled in the same car with us, the father choosing to stand near the door guarding his oversized luggage for the entire trip. The train made several stops along the way and a few enterprising salesmen hopped on to ride for one or two legs, possibly commuting home after a tough day pedaling sunglasses and umbrellas to tourists and unprepared locals. Some even had the knockoff designer purses Rick Steves warns his readers about. The salesmen used baby strollers as carts to carry their inventory on the train, each stroller piled high with large cardboard display boards and boxes of extra products. Dressed like con men in long coats and fedoras, their hip hugging jeans and DVS shoes fractured their image and confused the eye.

Arriving at Sorrento, the end of the tracks, we exited the train with our back packs and wheeled bags.

Before descending the stairs with the crowd I paused to gaze out the window, making sure I could see the sea and orient myself so I wouldn't have to read the map outside.

"You square? Do you need a taxi or anything?" The son of the LA family had apparently been sent by his parents, who stood near the elevator.

"No, we're good. Thank you. Enjoy your vacation!"

"You, too. And be safe," he ran to catch up to his parents, disappearing into the elevator.

We took the stairs, emerging into a warm, sunny evening smelling of the sea and fresh lemons. We walked one block and turned left on the main street and were immediately absorbed into a crowd that made the Napoli Centrale seem deserted. I'd never seen so many people on a street. We were all shoulder to shoulder, everyone walking at a fairly fast clip, making it impossible to carry on a conversation or even choose a direction with our backpacks and wheeled bags. Steph was ahead of me, parting the crowd by determination alone, glancing back every ten paces or so to make sure I was still behind her. My legs and feet were tired and the various stresses of the day were catching up to me, draining my energy. I worried I'd trip someone with my bag or knock someone down if I turned too quickly with my backpack. If someone fell here, they'd be trampled in no time.

"How much farther?" Steph called back to me.

"Keep going—we have to cross the square with all the flags," I answered. No flags were within sight yet, making it impossible to guess how far we had to walk. Our packs, probably heavier than they should have been when we started our vacation, had gained weight from our shopping trips thus far and presented an ever-increasing challenge for walking. We were shorter than most of the people ambling along beside us, forcing us to look upward to determine where we were heading. My stomach growled and sweat beaded on my forehead.

"How much farther?" Steph called back again.

"It's like a mile total—maybe we're halfway," I yelled back.

We finally reached Tasso Square, which also marked the end of the closed portion of the street, so we lumbered over to the sidewalk and continued on.

Finding our street was somewhat difficult as it crossed below the street we were on, had no street sign, and was accessed by a narrow concrete stairway branching off the sidewalk. A short walk along the street below delivered us to our hotel, the Ulisse Deluxe Hostel, where we checked in and collapsed on our bed, gratefully dropping our heavy packs on the floor.

Our spacious room featured a TV and telephone and a large bathroom complete with a bidet, but the lights only remained on for about two minutes before going off automatically. If we opened the door, the lights came back on. Shutting the door seemed to cause the lights to remain on for two minutes before going out again. We finally noticed a small card slot on the wall near the door and discovered sliding the key card into it activated the lights so they remained on, so when we left the room and removed the card key they would automatically extinguish and save electricity.

"Oh, so that's why they only gave us one key," said Steph.

Rick Steves suggests a restaurant on the waterfront, very close to our hotel. After asking directions at the front desk we set off in search of the shallow stairways and narrow pedestrian passageways to the wharf, where we found several restaurants and chose the first one that looked inviting, the tables inside with an open wall offering an expansive view of the marina. I ate spaghetti with prawns and Steph had spaghetti with tomatoes, reluctant to punish her stomach after a long day of snacks and a marathon luggage-hauling sprint to the hotel. For dessert I ordered a shot of Limoncello, the lemon liqueur on which Sorrento prides itself, and was rewarded with a clean lemon taste, no bitterness and just the right amount of sourness. Served in an ice cold glass, it was a fabulous finish to the meal and our exhausting day.

We sat a few minutes longer, gazing at the Isle of Capri (pronounced CAH-pree, quite the opposite of the way we hear it at home) and watching people amble about the marina, possibly going home to the apartments above the restaurants.

    Kate and Liam, we noted, should have arrived in their hotel by now, having taken a later train than we did. We'd exchanged hotel names before leaving Siena, Liam having chosen their Sorrento hotel for its location on the beach south of where we now rested.

Positano

Chapter Thirty-Four
Amalfi Coast
domenica (Sunday)

È tutto pepel.
He/she is all pepper.
(He/she is full of life.)

Reliving this trip as I sit at home writing about it fills me with a mad urge to begin planning our next European adventure, revisit our favorite places and rectify some of our first-timer mistakes. Our next trip will include Pisa and Cinque Terre, but I hope we somehow include Sorrento again because our experience there was the worst part of the trip.

The town itself is beautiful, featuring palm trees and lemon trees, flowers blooming and perfuming, wisteria draped over arbors and hanging seductively above archways, white buildings proudly lining the streets. Perched on the edge of the Mediterranean Sea, the Isle of Capri provides a scenic view and a worthy tourist attraction.

Our plans for the day began with boarding a bus that would carry us south along the ocean's edge on a hairpin highway carved into the side of the cliffs. Rick Steves calls this "one of the all-time great white-knuckle rides"; in my opinion, an understatement. Stephanie was less than enthusiastic.

"This is stupid," she said as the bus careened to a stop to allow an oncoming car, spied in the mirror positioned on the first sharp turn, to pass. The car passed and our bus resumed its carnival ride, sailing around curves and up and down hills seemingly without regard for safety or worries about failing brakes. The waves crashed far below us as we continued on, one of only a few vehicles on the road on this Easter Sunday, cruising through short tunnels and turning so sharply it seemed we'd meet ourselves and get stuck in an endless loop. The bus driver stomped forcefully on the gas and brake as if he were killing bugs. Unable to capture the true majesty of the Amalfi Coast highway with my camera, I continued to snap photos hoping for at least one good shot.

We hopped off (escaped?) the bus at the first stop, Positano, to explore the town.

Positano is a vertical town, perched on a cliff with two small beaches at the water's edge. The view from the bus stop is incredible: rooftops, flowers, lemon trees, a sliver of beach, and the Mediterranean Sea. Behind the town the cliffs rise up, brushing against the sky and snagging clouds, stretching them into thin veils.

There are two roads in Positano: the highway, stretching along the edge of the cliffs from town to town on the Amalfi Coast, and a winding, one-way street that wends crazily from one end of town to the other. The rest of the streets are narrow concrete walkways and stairways built into the side of the cliff.

This was the first day warm enough to wear capris and sandals, which is what we did. After snapping several photos from the lofty perch of the bus stop we chose a path and started toward the beach. This day would live in my memory as the single most perfect day of our trip as we explored Positano, discovering the pedestrian lane lined with shops selling everything from art to ceramics to clothing and shoes, custom-made while you wait. The beach sand was coarse and dark due to the presence of volcanic lava, and it exfoliated our feet as we waded and collected sea glass, little pieces of light glinting from the dark sand.

"We're wading in the Mediterranean Sea!" Steph remarked, grinning.

"It's Easter Sunday and we are relaxing on the Amalfi Coast," I replied. The beach featured about a hundred lounge chairs, each with its own sun shade, so we rested for a while before venturing along the cliffside walkway, my jacket pockets bulging with sea glass and small pebbles.

The ferry to Sorrento had already sailed by the time I checked the schedule, so we decided to start walking back toward the bus stop and eat lunch along the way. We watched for Kate and Liam but had no real idea which restaurant they would choose and we didn't find them in Positano.

The walkway we found appeared new and ran along the side of the cliff, intersecting with other pedestrian streets every now and then. We paused a few times to take photos and comment on this perfect day, noticing the scented air (a heady mixture of exotic flowers and lemons with a slight tinge of fresh sea air) and wishing we could somehow preserve the smell. Gazing straight down at the sea was dizzying and we only met a handful of people, all tourists, on the walkway. Eventually we came upon a pizza place tucked into the cliff, up one flight of stairs from the walkway.

Maybe we were especially hungry after walking all day, or maybe the Mediterranean air makes food taste better than usual, but we agreed this pizza was the best we'd had on the entire trip. We ordered it with Buffalo mozzarella, black olives and capers. The olives hadn't been pitted but we ate them anyway, marveling at the view.

After lunch we continued to the second, smaller beach to resume our quest for sea glass and interesting bits of worn pottery shards. At the far end of the beach a stairway led upward and we began our ascent to the bus stop.

The steps! There are easily 1000 steps from the beach to the highway in this vertical town. We met no one on our climb, which we likened to Olympic training as we wondered if our thighs were growing as we marched up and up and up. We passed by scenic vistas, beneath arbors, around giant cacti and past interesting gates and doorways to residences marked with decorative ceramic address plaques. As we climbed I wondered if my knees and ankles would buckle under the strain. I wondered if anyone had ever expired here, mid-climb, and how the ambulance crew would carry the stretcher around these tight corners and up the steep flights.

Small green lizards entertained us during our brief pauses, darting in and out between rocks, seeking sun and security. The treasures in my jacket pockets became heavier with each flight of stairs but I was determined to carry them home as tangible evidence of our presence on the Mediterranean beach. I checked on them to make sure the pockets would withstand the strain of the added weight, and the sea glass emitted a comforting glow. *I'm carrying a pocketful of light*, I thought.

Finally staggering to the bus stop, we met two women waiting for the next bus to Sorrento. I'd hoped to see more of the Amalfi Coast, but Steph didn't want to spend any more time on the bus and we'd stayed later than planned, leaving little time for exploring other towns, so we decided to head back to the hotel. Our bus presently paused, the new bus driver demonstrating a more sedate style than the one who'd delivered us there that morning. All the way back to Sorrento, he slowed for every blind corner and honked his horn three or four times before proceeding.

The bus ride provided enough respite for Steph's legs, but mine still felt leaden as we walked to our hotel from the bus stop. After a brief nap we gathered our clothes and walked to the laundromat, two blocks and one flight of stairs away.

Sitting in the launderette we watched a neverending stream of cars the size of dog houses whiz by. We laundered in solitude until a local man came in to wash his clothes and establish himself on an adjacent chair.

"Ciao," he nodded and smiled.

"Ciao. Parla inglese?" I responded.

"Si, yes. I thought you looked like Americans," he nodded again.

"You're right, we are. Do you live here in Sorrento?"

"I do now, yes. With my father. I am—how you say—between jobs at this particular moment."

"What kind of job are you looking for?"

"I'm not looking right now, just taking care of my father and working on my..." he flexed his arm, pointing to his bicep. "Arm muscle here. What is it you call this muscle here?"

"That's your bicep. So you're lifting weights?"

"Bicep, yes. I lift the weights each day at dawn."

I asked him a few questions about Sorrento and learned the average house costs between €700,000 and €1,000,000 and in his opinion the local wages aren't high enough to support these prices.

We wrestled our laundry back to the hotel and left in search of dinner, once again gravitating to the marina. The crowds seemed to center on the main street of town from Tasso Square north, so our little corner of the city enjoyed a slightly less hectic pace.

The restaurant we chose offered a spectacular view of Capri and the waiter brought us complimentary shots of Limoncello. It's not customary to tip in Italy but we left an extra €4 to thank him for his preferential treatment.

Feeling more confident in our navigational skills, we took a different route back to the hotel and didn't get lost.

My feet ached when we reached our room and I looked forward to an evening of loafing with elevated feet. I'd just settled into a comfortable position when our phone rang. Startled, we both froze and stared at each other for a few seconds.

"I haven't heard a phone ring in over a week," said Steph, picking it up. *"Pronto,"* she answered in Italian style.

It was Liam.

"We're in the lobby," he said. "Can we come up to your room?"

Kate and Liam appeared at our door a moment later, regaling us with their train schedule troubles the day before and sharing their Amalfi Coast adventure. They'd never found the lost camera. We told them about the fake porter in Napoli and the crude remarks some of the men called out to us as we walked along the street.

"What are you doing tomorrow?" Kate asked.

"We're thinking about taking the ferry to Capri, checking out the island, maybe touring the Blue Grotto," I said. "What about you two?"

"We're hanging out at the beach in front of our hotel. After yesterday's crazy train schedule and today's buses and all the walking and exploring, we need a day to kick back," she said.

"If you don't take the ferry, you can come and hang out with us," Liam invited, grinning.

"Yes, feel free to drop in on us. I know Liam is getting tired of my company," Kate smiled.

"Oh no, Mom, it's not that I'm tired of your company; I just want more company," he looked over at us. "I crave people. I always want people around me. The more people, the happier I am."

"I know," Kate ruffled his hair. "It's true, he loves having people around."

We made plans to meet the next evening for

dinner. Kate and Liam would choose a restaurant and let us know where to meet them. They were leaving for Rome a day before we were, and dropped a casual invitation for us to accompany them to Pompeii and on to Rome if we wanted to cut our Sorrento visit short.

After our visitors left we called home for a quick chat before collapsing on the bed and sleeping like the weary travelers we were.

The Isle of Capri

Chapter Fifty-Five
Sorrento
Day of Disenchantment
lunedí (Monday)

Diciamo pane al pane e vino al vino.
Let's say bread for bread and wine for wine.
(Let's call a spade a spade.)

Easter Monday is a national holiday in Italy, observed as a three-day weekend from most corporate jobs, and many Napolese travel south to Sorrento for a few days. Apparently this town, at the last train stop, attracts all the loud, rude, crude, pushy people.

We walked the streets after enjoying our breakfast buffet, a map clutched in my hand as we searched for the ferry to Capri. A slight breeze teased the palm trees and stirred the lemons, enhancing the morning air with the distinctive Amalfi scents. It seemed no matter where we walked, groups of men called out crude remarks as we passed by.

Sometimes we had to step off the sidewalk to allow men to continue forward, even while calling us lewd names and leering threateningly. I remembered reading in Rick Steves' books and website about the Italian men: although they feel compelled to announce their private thoughts and intimidate women with their remarks, they rarely commit acts of violence.

"Just ignore them, Steph. They won't hurt us, they're just being rude." The only fair-haired girls on the street, it was as if we had a spotlight trained on us. Tiring of the incessant insults and missing our turn to the ferry dock, we returned to our room for a brief period of quiet, hoping to calm our nerves and heal from the verbal assaults.

By the time we located the ferry (the narrow stairway to a lower street had previously been hidden by the milling crowds) it was time for lunch. We purchased our ferry tickets and ate on the second floor, or first *piano*, of a restaurant on the ferry dock. Three women at a nearby table heard us speaking English and introduced themselves, asking about our travel plans.

"I'm here for a semester in Rome," explained the youngest one. "and my mom and aunt came to visit for Easter. Are you enjoying your vacation? Have you been to Rome yet?"

"Not yet—that's our next stop. We're having

fun overall," I told them, "but the men are pretty vocal."

"Especially here," said Steph. "They're really rude."

"That's too bad, I'm sorry you have to put up with that. They won't hurt you, though. They mainly like yelling and gesturing, especially from across the street."

"I hope Rome is nicer than this place," said Steph.

"Oh, I love Rome. It's fabulous. And make sure you notice the graffiti. It's all positive graffiti and words about loved ones who've died, like memorials to friends and so on. I thought the graffiti was scary until I learned what it says."

"That's interesting," Steph smiled.

"Yeah, and there aren't as many men just walking around staring and yelling. It's a big city, so everyone has things to do. It's a city of workers, so everyone is rushing someplace. I promise, you'll like it there." We thanked her and wished her well as they left, and we headed for the ferry to explore the intriguing Isle of Capri.

The breeze, gently wafting seductive Mediterranean scents on land, became nearly gale force on the water, casually tossing the large ferry from wave to wave, occasionally dropping it into a violent rocking motion in the deep troughs. The passenger cabin was only about a quarter full, people filling the vomit bags and children screaming and crying in fright.

It seemed to take two hours to arrive in Capri but my phone indicated only 45 minutes had passed. We debarked the ferry quickly, eager to walk on solid land and gulp fresh air, only to enter a stew of disorganization on the wide cement dock. We were squeezed up against the cement wall, hundreds of people standing on each other's feet, breathing each other's air, pressing into everyone in a nearly intimate manner. I clutched my purse, slung across my body and underneath my jacket, thinking if a pick pocket were nimble enough to move in this crazy crush, he'd become wealthy in moments. A cacophony of foreign languages and the occasional partial siren wail added an intimidating factor to the experience. We maintained eye contact, having barely lost touch of each other in the jumble of bodies, as a tiny ambulance inched its way by barely two feet from the wall into which my shoulder blades were grinding. The emergency vehicle headed toward the Island, probably returning from a previous run, and its painfully slow passage finally ended when it passed us and we could peel ourselves from the masses.

"Are you okay?" asked a middle-aged woman, rounding up her relatives. "You look pale."

"No, no, we're fine. *Grazie*," we replied, glancing at each other.

The wind howled around Capri, causing the

Blue Grotto to cancel all tours. We decided not to ride the funicular, a slightly terrifying ride on a sunny, still day but unimaginably crippling on a day like this. Crowds milled around along the boardwalk but no one seemed overtly lewd like they had in Sorrento. We bought ferry tickets back to the mainland and browsed through the shops near the dock, treating ourselves to gelato and snapping photos of Capri's majestic mountains and marina.

Unsure how quickly we could locate our ferry and traverse the dock, we proceeded out along the breakwall and boarded early, which turned out to be our one lucky act of the day. As soon as we boarded they shut the doors, over capacity and offering standing room only. Steph and I stationed ourselves near the door, clutching a handrail and commiserating about our day.

"Even Mother Nature doesn't like us today," said Steph. "I'm glad we have dinner with Kate and Liam to look forward to."

"Yeah, that'll be great. We'll have time to relax in our room for a few minutes before dinner so we can freshen up and get ready."

"Where are you from?" asked a young guy near my elbow. He appeared Italian, dark hair and dark eyes with a very impressive camera hanging from a neck strap under his long black jacket.

Steph enunciated slowly and clearly, "We are from the Yoo-Nite-Ed States."

"Yeah, I know that. I'm from Ohio," he grinned. "But where are you from?"

"Oh. Michigan. The Upper Peninsula," Steph grinned.

"Oh, I know where that is. I'm in college, over here for ten days for a photography course."

"Did you go up in the funicular on Capri?" I asked.

"Yep, but it was pretty hairy. They shut the Blue Grotto tours down so we didn't get to go there. I'm exhausted—no one is sleeping on this trip because we're seeing and doing so much every day. I'm going back to the room early to take a nap right now."

He'd thought Steph was in college, and was surprised to learn she's still in 10th grade. We told him about our trip and wished him well as we arrived at the Sorrento dock a mere twenty minutes after leaving Capri.

"Amazing what a difference a tail wind makes," remarked the Ohio student as we scattered from the dock.

Upon returning to the hotel, I asked for the Internet password and spent an hour finding a reservation for an extra night in Rome. We cancelled our last night in Sorrento and planned to accompany

Liam and Kate to Pompeii, arriving in Rome a day earlier than planned.

The hotel clerk was very understanding. "It's not always like this," she explained in her impeccable English. "It's the Napoli men—they have a long weekend and they come down here and cause trouble. If you stay another day it won't be like it was today."

"I'm sure you're right," I told her, "but we're ready to go. We're meeting friends in Rome."

As I sat in the lobby searching for a hotel on my phone, about a dozen children ran back and forth screeching in Italian, chasing each other in some version of tag. My head pounded from the day's stressors: the lewd remarks, the wind, the crush on the dock, and now the shrill untethered children racing by, their voices echoing off the walls.

A woman approached the front desk, speaking slowly in a snooty British accent. "Excuse me," she began, staring down her nose at the seated clerk. "Is there any way you can tell these *lovely* children," she gestured vaguely, waving one hand palm-up to encompass the entire lobby.

"...to shut up?" asked the clerk, winking.

"Yes!" She stepped back, moving her hand to her chest and lowering her voice. "I mean, yes. Please."

"Absolutely, madam." He grabbed the next miscreant sprinting by and told him something in rapid, stern Italian that caused them to walk silently to the nearest couch and sit down, staring balefully at the other guests.

I finally completed the booking process for the first night in Rome, at a hotel two doors down from the one we had already booked for the following night. Our first night in Rome would cost €80, and the second night (already paid for before we left home) was €180. The bother of transferring our luggage from one hotel to another was worth the €100 savings. We would stay Tuesday night in the cheaper place, then carry our bags down the street and stay Wednesday night at the Mecenate Palace, a luxury hotel I'd been looking forward to since I first booked the room.

Liam called from the lobby, ready to escort us to dinner. "Mom's meeting us at the restaurant. I told her I could find your hotel and find the restaurant again. It's easy," he explained, holding the door so we could step out into the balmy evening.

We ate at *La Fenice*, a restaurant Kate had found. It offered a friendly, boisterous atmosphere as a perfect antidote to our day and we relaxed right into the scene the moment we walked through the door.

"Drinks for you?" asked the waiter. Kate and I each ordered vino.

"Umm, do you have sodapop here?" asked Liam.

"Sodapop? Like your granddad? No, granddad is not here," the waiter grinned. "Drink?"

"You have to say Fanta," Steph reminded Liam.

"Oh, right. Do you have Fanta?"

"We have *fawn-tah*," the waiter over-pronounced, still grinning and winking at the kids. "Is that what you want? Fawn-tah?"

"*Si*," said Liam.

"And you?" he asked Steph.

"I would like a Fanta. Do you have flavors, or just orange?"

"Orange is a flavor," he laughed. "And it's the flavor of our *Fawn-tah*."

"Okay, I'll have that, then."

We ordered our meals: Linguine with Seafood for Kate and me, Four-Cheese Macaroni for Liam and Spaghetti with Clams for Steph. Our conversation never flagged as we discussed our respective experiences in Italy so far, brief outlines of our life stories, and touched on political affiliation. Kate is a democrat but I told her I won't hold that against her as many of my close friends are democrats and we just avoid discussing politics. "Okay by me," she smiled. "I don't like discussing politics anyway."

"Neither do I," I agreed.

I told them both about this book and my plans for writing it when we return to the States and they both gave permission before I'd even asked to use their first names and mail them each a copy of the finished product. Sitting in my office today writing these words evokes the entire evening. I hope the four of us will somehow meet again.

"So how bad were the comments the guys were saying to you?" asked Liam.

Steph looked uncertain about repeating the coarse words. "They were very graphic and crude," I said.

"That's not right. I don't know why boys and men have to treat women that way," said Liam.

"That's because you're a good guy," said Kate. "You would never treat anyone like that. Did you notice how angry the Italian women seem? I feel like every local woman I see walking on the street is frowning at the sidewalk, stomping along like she's mad at the world."

"Yes, I did notice that, now that you mention it. They're probably just tired of the men making comments," said Steph.

"That really bothers me the way they were talking to you guys," said Liam.

"Well, there's nothing you can do about that, but you can make sure you keep treating everyone the way you know they should be treated," said Kate. Liam nodded.

We told Kate and Liam we'd booked a room in Rome so we could accompany them to Pompeii the next day on the way to Rome, and they were delighted.

"We'll meet you at the train station around 9:30 tomorrow morning," said Kate.

"Oh, we're Type A—we'll be there at 9:15," I grinned at her.

"Well, we'll be there around 9:30," she twirled her finger in a circular motion as we all laughed.

"I'm smiling a lot right now because we are going to join you guys tomorrow morning," said Liam.

"The rest of our trip just took a turn for the better," I said.

The waiter posed for a photo with the kids before we paid our tab and exited the restaurant, walking back to our hotel with Kate and Liam before they continued on to their own to pack and prepare for our Pompeiian tour the next morning.

Mt. Vesuvius viewed from Pompeii

Chapter Eighty-Nine
Pompeii, Roma
martedí (Tuesday)

Ha molto sale in zucca.
He/She has a lot of salt in his/her pumpkin.
(He/She has a lot of good sense.)

Eager to leave the next morning, we allowed plenty of time for our slow, cumbersome walk to the train station and decided to stop at an English restaurant for breakfast to avoid arriving embarrassingly early. Kate and Liam spied us from across the street and we walked together from there.

"Mom figured out why the Italian ladies look so angry all the time," Liam skipped along backwards in front of us.

"What did she determine?"

"They're all tired of the men shouting obscene

things and making rude gestures," explained Kate. "They're tired of feeling like a piece of meat."

This seemed plausible, given our recent exposure to particularly boorish behavior. "I think you're right," I agreed.

Steph nodded along. "At least we get to go back home. Imagine living here all the time with those men! They shouldn't even be called men. They're more like animals."

We bought a train ticket to Pompeii, a short ride from Sorrento, and stood in a passenger-filled train all the way there. An older gentleman with swarthy skin serenaded us with his saxophone, virtually shortening the ride. The air outside the train window was seasonably warm, the brazen sun highlighting everything in bas relief. I wore my trusty sandals, inviting ancient Pompeiian dust to decorate my feet.

The list of facts I knew about Pompeii before our visit was abysmally short: it was an ancient city obliterated by a volcanic eruption and buried in lava, and was later excavated and discovered as a completely intact city. I had no idea it was so large and well laid out, or that it presented evidence of a technologically advanced society boasting sophisticated inventions such as a gravity-fed municipal water system and artfully intricate tile floors. This lack of knowledge suppressed my enthusiasm a bit, but may have also contributed to my unexpected wonder.

Steph acted as our Pompeiian tour guide,

reading aloud from the Rick Steves guide book and directing us through town past all of the interesting sights. We spent a few hours imagining a day-to-day existence in this ancient city, appreciating the Roman tradition of 'eating out' at the lunch counters (Pompeiians rarely cooked their own meals), sitting on the carved stone theatre seats to envision a live performance, and pausing for a moment of reverential silence in the brothel, decorated with crudely explicit drawings depicting various sexual positions (a primitive list of options?). The brutal lifestyle of the prostitutes is heartbreaking to imagine; the worn concrete beds stopped my breath.

Liam enjoyed walking on the stepping stones whenever possible, admiring the ruts left in the roads by the horse drawn carts, and comparing the elaborate details of the water fountains. The four of us took turns posing for photos in the Forum, the bakery, the House of the Faun and other ruins.

We paused for a snack in the modern-day cafeteria near the center of Pompeii and checked the route we'd traveled through town. Satisfied we'd seen everything listed by Rick Steves, we proceeded to claim our luggage and buy our tickets to Napoli.

Once again we were on the platform when we realized we hadn't stamped our train tickets. After a moment of panic while Liam sprinted down the stairs, through the hall and up the stairs to the station, then returned to the platform, we were ready for the next leg of our journey.

The Napoli train station proved just as congested as the first time we'd been there, but less intimidating since we were part of a larger party this time and no one approached us to 'help' locate our next connection. The kids guarded the bags while Kate and I tried to purchase tickets through a vending machine, but it wouldn't sell us the tickets we needed. The tellers selling tickets behind the counter were facing a zig-zagging line of approximately 250 people.

"I'll stand in line and buy the tickets if you want to keep the kids company," offered Kate. "You can just pay me for your tickets once I get them."

"Sounds good to me," I said, leaving Kate at the tail end of the line while I rejoined the kids, standing guard over our huge pile of luggage. Liam had an inflatable soccer ball, perfect for kicking lightly up in the air and bouncing off his head until a security guard stopped by and told him this type of activity wasn't allowed. He quickly revamped the game, sitting on the floor and creating a corridor with the luggage, Stephanie at the other end, so they could roll the ball back and forth between them. The security guard still wasn't happy but he didn't have enough imagination to think of a reason to stop this game.

I kept one eye on Kate, progressing through the line at a glacial speed. Eventually she emerged from the crowd, four train tickets to Roma held victoriously in her hand and a grin on her face.

"The slow train was cheaper, but full. The fast train cost twice as much, but it goes twice as fast, and it leaves in twenty minutes," she explained.

"Great! Let's run. I'll pay you when we get on board," I said, grabbing random bags and starting toward the platforms.

We found our seats, but one of them was already occupied. We conferred, double checked the seat numbers, the date and train number on the tickets. Finally the man sitting in the seat spoke.

"It's me. I'm not supposed to be here. I made a mistake," he spoke slowly to compensate for his accent. "I bought my ticket but it's for tomorrow. I meant for it to be for today. We are riding together." He gestured toward his friend, "and I work tomorrow. I hope they let me stay on here."

"It's not like you're cheating the system," I said, hoping to make him feel better. "You're still paying and there's obviously room for you on this train." I gestured across the aisle to a few empty seats.

"Yes, I'll sit over there and see what happens," he agreed, looking defeated as he shuffled over and settled into a different seat.

"Have you guys ridden on the fast train before?" asked Liam.

"No, we've had all slow trains here so far," I replied.

"Us, too. I'm excited to see how fast this baby goes." The train started rolling, leaving Napoli and Mt.

Vesuvius behind.

I handed Kate a wad of Euros for the train tickets. "I'm so glad you chose the fast train," I told her. "We're running out of vacation, so I'd rather pay more and do more at this point."

"Well, that's what I was thinking," said Kate. "It's worth it at this point. I figured we've seen enough of Napoli Centrale."

As I write this, months later and half a world away, I shut my eyes to fully envision the scene: The landscape whizzing by below us, the cacophony of conversations on the train, Kate's tired smile, my own lethargy, the kids fighting sleep across the aisle. I gaze out the window, desperately trying to capture this moment, this scenery, and hold it forever intact in my mind. One of my worst habits is living in the future, forever anticipating and planning for the next event or obligation, and I rarely sit back and just experience the moment. My goal for this vacation was to do just that, and I think I have. I concentrate on the tiny towns and green trees gliding by and reflect on my capacity for living in the moment on this trip. I congratulate myself on attaining this level of presence, just like Eckhardt Tolle postulates in *A New Earth*. Yes, I think, Eckhardt would be proud of my progress. He would recognize the transition I've made from constant planner/preparer and future liver to present liver. Liver? I ask myself, chuckling inwardly. Kate looks at me and I realize I actually chuckled aloud at my own musings. She's carrying on an interesting conversation with the man sitting across the aisle, a lanky, pale, clean cut man from Bologna who just spent the weekend with family in Naples. She's asking him about drinking in Italy.

"So if there's no drinking age, do you have problems over here with alcohol? In the States people are always getting arrested or thrown in jail for driving drunk."

"No, not so much drinking over here. Everyone drinks, and everyone can so it's not as exciting. But we have such good transportation, like this train, so we don't have to drive as much as you do." He's in a band and has traveled several times to the States to perform, in Denver, Boston, LA and several other cities.

"One thing people do over here," he continues, "is correct our buzz." He glanced at us and grinned, "so we'll have an espresso after dinner, but it's too late in the evening for that, it will keep us awake, so then we correct it with a grappa."

"Grappa? Is that alcohol?" asks Kate.

"Yes, if you haven't had grappa, you need to try it. It's very strong, made from grapes. Like a grape liquor."

I pull out my Rick Steves phrase book to look up grappa, and there it is, listed in the Menu Decoder section, right across from its English translation: firewater.

"We'll have to order one with dinner," says Kate.

"Let's share it," I point to the phrase book.

"Yes, let's," she agrees, turning toward our new friend. "You speak English very well," Kate tells him.

"Well, I try. I've been to the States so many times, I should by now," he laughs. "I'm actually trying to move over there. I just have to get my paperwork straight before I do it."

Kate is incredulous. "You want to move there? But it's beautiful here. Why would you want to live over there?"

"It's beautiful here, yes. But preservation, living with all of these ancient things, it gets old," we laugh, waiting for him to go on. "For example, if you want to build something, it takes forever to get permits. They must make sure nothing was ever on the sight on which you want to build. Once you get the permits and start working, digging and excavating, if you find something, anything, like a piece of a column or a chunk of marble that may have been a cornice, all work stops while they file more permits and bring in experts to dig and remove all the remains properly," he waves his hands, dismissing the whole process. "It's tedious. Very extremely tedious."

"So it gets old, living with old things," says Kate.

He laughs. "*Sì*, yes."

I relax and let the conversations wash over me, listening from afar, observing the train trundling faithfully north on the only path available to it, rushing toward Roma.

The man who'd been sitting in our seats was evicted at the one stop between Napoli and Roma after a protracted argument with the ticket agent.

"What will you do?" I asked him.

"I'll have to leave the train. It's my fault," he shrugged. "I shouldn't have boarded it in Napoli."

"Maybe you can hop back on a later train," I whispered.

He smiled. "*Sì*, that is my plan. I'll still get to Bologna."

The Roma Termini station boasts a well-organized layout. We easily made our way to the front of the station and outside. Our hotels were in two different directions, but each one was only two or three blocks from the station.

"Let's just meet back here in two hours," said Kate.

"Okay, it's easy to find, that should work out," I replied. "Then we'll go to dinner."

"I'm taking us to the restaurant where Mom and I ate when we first came to Italy," announced Liam.

"Can you find it again?" I asked.

"It's right by the Spanish Steps. I remember exactly. And you have to have the Tiramisu for dessert!" He instructed.

"Well, I don't know about that, but we're definitely up for dinner," Steph grinned at him, hoisting her bag on her shoulders. "Let's go find our hotel so we can drop off these bags."

Our hotel was three blocks from the Termini Station. Three blocks of broken, congested sidewalks over which we dragged our wheeled bags, stopping every few seconds to right them when they flipped to their sides on the heaved sidewalk cracks. The doorways were clogged with people wearing surly expressions and dirty clothes. They forced us to step onto the street to get around them while they trained their disdainful gazes just above our heads. Most people appeared to be Asian in this section of the city and they stared boldly as we struggled by.

Our low expectations for the hotel on this, our first night in The Eternal City, were tidily met and surpassed by the welcoming staff and clean but cramped room. The shower was a stand-up stall sized for a six-year-old; we decided to wait until checking into the luxury hotel the following night to shower.

We had time for a brief rest and a pause at the ATM across the street before navigating the unwelcoming route back to the Termini Station. We loitered in front of the doors for a few minutes before Liam's blue sweatshirt popped into sight as he jogged toward us.

"Are you ready to see Rome?" he bounded up, gesturing behind him. "Mom's coming. She told me to run ahead and find you."

"Great! Let's go find your restaurant," I said.

"Are you going to order the Tiramisu for dessert?" He skipped and bounced ahead, spinning around to address me. "It's the best dessert in Italy."

"I'm seriously considering it."

We joined Kate and began walking in the general direction of the Spanish Steps.

"Rome isn't as big as you think," said Kate. "Once you walk around it you realize it's an easy city to get around and you cover more ground than you expect."

"It's safe, too," Liam added. "We didn't have any troubles when we were here before."

"We aren't traveling with a beautiful teenaged girl, either," Kate said. "That brings a whole new facet to the situation."

"Well, we are now, but I'm not going to allow any remarks from rude people," said Liam.

The Spanish Steps are grand: two sweeping staircases, each consisting of 138 steps, wide and short, connecting two piazzas. A modern-day meeting and resting place, it's difficult to capture this sight on film without hordes of people crowding the frame. We walked up one side of the Steps and stood, surveying the scene below and watching people (one mother was counting each step in an excited voice while her young daughter marched alongside, reciting the numbers *una, due, trei, quattro...*). I noticed someone in my peripheral vision suddenly run over to us and tap my shoulder, startling me.

"I just wanted to say hey," he said. "We rode the same train this morning. How was Pompeii? Was it solid?" I remembered his face then, and his group of four or five people. They'd been in the same area on the train, standing near us at the back of the car while we listened to the saxophone.

"Pompeii was fabulous. I thought you looked familiar. Is everyone enjoying Rome so far?"

"Yeah, it's great. Well, I recognized you and wanted to say hello. They're waiting for me—take care."

"You, too. Enjoy the rest of your trip."

Liam's restaurant was just a few paces from the bottom of the Spanish Steps. He requested a table in the back and we were seated immediately at a spacious table in a private room at the rear of the restaurant. We ate a leisurely meal complete with cappuccino, wine, and tiramisu for dessert. Liam wasn't exaggerating; the tiramisu was truly spectacular.

"This is probably the best day of my whole trip," said Liam. "We ate breakfast in Sorrento, lunch in Pompeii and dinner in Rome."

While we ate dinner and chatted with the waitress, evening descended outside.

Rome at night is a sight to behold. We paused at the Trevi Fountain to wish for safe travels, snapping photos that would never do the grand, intricate carving justice. From there we continued to a few tourist shops, stopping to watch a few street entertainers and artists, tossing a coin into their collections.

Liam was searching for a dagger. "Here's the store Mom and I shopped in a couple weeks ago!"

We walked into a narrow store featuring shelves crammed with merchandise ranging from cheap key chains to designer leather purses, shields, paper weights, tote bags and daggers. Steph found a purse she liked with a prohibitive price tag of €45.

"Mom, check out this purse. It's really nice but it's forty-five Euros! Isn't it cool, though?" She tried it on, walking around the display shelves.

"Mom and I were in here a couple weeks ago and I bought a dagger. I bet they remember me here. I'll see if I can get you a deal," said Liam. He started talking to the salesman, who came over to negotiate with Steph. Apparently he wanted to sell the purse so they could close the store on a lucky note.

"Your brother says you want this purse," the salesman gestured toward the purse on Steph's shoulder.

"My brother? Oh, yes, he's my brother. Yes, I'm interested in the purse. I really like it but it's forty-five Euros."

"What you think it should cost? How about thirty-five Euros?"

"Umm, well, thirty-five is better than forty-five but it's still too much," Steph's negotiating skills had improved a hundred fold since we landed in Venice two short weeks ago.

"What you think of thirty Euros? That enough savings for you? I only give you this deal because of your brother," the salesman gestured at Liam, grinning at each of us in turn. "He was a good customer."

Steph held the purse out, considering, then placed it on her shoulder again. "Yes, I'll take it for thirty."

We continued on down the street, enjoying the festival atmosphere of Rome at night, until we reached the intersection of Quattro Fontaine and Settembre. This intersection featured four intricately carved fountains, one on each corner, and it was the logical place for us to split so Kate and Liam could continue on to their hotel and we to ours. They would leave the next morning, so this was our final farewell.

"Good luck to you guys," said Kate, hugging both of us.

"Safe travels home," we replied. Saying goodbye was bittersweet at best; Steph and I both knew our last day in Rome wouldn't be as fun without our travel companions.

We reached our hotel a few minutes later and tossed and turned all night, each of us too tired to relax and sleep. The street noises weren't as intrusive as I'd expected but my weary feet kept me awake.

Typical Roman architecture

Chapter One Hundred Forty-Four
Roma
mercoledí (Wednesday)

Sta facendo il pappagallo.
He/She is making like a parrot.
(He/She is repeating everything verbatim.)

The sirens outside gradually penetrated my consciousness, so when I actively noticed and recognized the sounds I realized they'd been squealing for hours. The festive siren tune, a jaunty three-note trill followed by a longer, flatter note, seems to alert pedestrians and motorists of a madcap party, something on the order of Alice in Wonderland, rather than trauma or emergency.

"What's going on? It sounds like a million sirens," said Steph as I walked toward the window.

"They're not on our street; they must be

whizzing around the circle a half-block away."

We packed our bags and checked out of the hotel, hauling our belongings three doors down and struggling through the gold revolving doors of the Mecenate Palace. The concierge studied us with a disdainful stare above his reading glasses, taking in our rumpled appearances, our apparent exhaustion, our non-designer luggage. I wondered if I had dirt on my face or if he gazed at everyone with such condescension, and mentally dubbed him Snooty McSnootpants in an effort to maintain my somewhat ragged humor.

"Can I…help you?" he pursed his lips.

I drew myself up to a regal posture to match his and tried to enliven my tired face with a big smile. "We have reservations for tonight and we're wondering if you can hold our bags until we can check in."

He regarded our bags, no doubt wondering why he was forced to pander to street people who'd most likely spent the night on a bench somewhere. "I suppose you can leave your…luggage," he sighed, snapping his fingers to summon the bellhop. A tall, skinny man with thinning hair and a wide grin suddenly appeared from the next room to tag our bags and move them to the storage area, assuring us they'd be safe until we returned. Mr. McSnootpants maintained his boorish attitude as he focused on the bellhop's exposed wrists, which extended well beyond the edge of his jacket cuffs when he reached out to grasp our bags.

"At least they speak English," Steph whispered.

"And they provide an entertaining show," I answered.

"You may return after fifteen-thirty to…access your room," announced Mr. McSnootpants as I signed the receipt.

"Thank you. Do you have internet access here?"

"It is available in our lobby. Would you like the information? It isn't…free," he said.

"How much does it cost?"

"Five Euros every thirty minutes," his insincere grin reminded me of Kah, the snake with hypnotic eyes in the Jungle Book movie.

"Okay, I'll let you know if we need it," I said. The price worked out to fifteen dollars per hour at this, the most expensive hotel on our trip. The cheaper hotels had offered free internet access. I wondered what other surprises were in store for us at this palace.

We left the hotel free of our bags to take a circuitous route past the pyramid to the Spanish Steps to take some photos for Liam, as he'd requested. Suffering from sore, tired legs and feet we plodded down side streets, working our way toward the pyramid before we emerged on the major streets that intersect along two sides of it.

Steph quickly figured out how to cross Roman streets: with a fearless, confident attitude she strode across the first lane of traffic, staring down the drivers in the second lane until they paused to let us by. Several times I would wait for an opportunity to cross and end up jogging to catch up with her as she stood on the center line glaring at the motorists.

"Why are we walking to this pyramid? Can we go inside?" asked Steph.

"No, we can just see it from outside and take pictures. It's a real crypt, built on the same scale as the pyramids in Egypt."

"That's fascinating, Mom," Steph was starting to sound like Mr. McSnootpants.

"Not everyone who visits Rome sees this pyramid, or even knows it's here."

"I wonder why," she sighed.

After photographing the pyramid we continued on along the river, our feet protesting with each step. We stopped at a gelateria for a snack and a brief rest, paying four Euros for one scoop of gelato.

"The sign says it's only three Euros," Steph pointed out.

"I'm too tired to argue. I'll just pay four," I told her, handing the man behind the counter the exact change. "Let's sit outside for a minute while you eat, and rest our feet."

We sat in the sun, preparing to watch the cars and people streaming by, when the man suddenly appeared from behind the counter to yell at us. "No sit! No sit!" he shooed us away with frantic waves of his arms. "Is different price to sit. Take away. You go."

We were the only customers in the entire place, clearly not taking up room for any higher-paying clients, but again I was too tired to argue. We scrambled across the street to perch on the bottom steps of the Campidoglio and continued to watch large groups of tourists following their guides like gaggles of geese, straying off and returning, talking amongst themselves and missing most of the guides' lectures.

Finally reaching the Spanish Steps, we took several shots for Liam before perching on the edge, refusing to purchase roses from several men trolling up and down the stairs. I'd wanted to see the Borghese Gardens next but exhaustion was becoming impossible to ignore so we returned to our hotel early to find Mr. McSnootpants had been replaced by someone with a more agreeable personality who was willing to let us into our room prior to check-in time.

Our room, far from palatial, featured fabric-covered walls decorated with suspicious black spots along the corners from floor to ceiling, threadbare chairs and wobbly-legged tables. The fridge was stocked with various snacks and drinks, each with a royal price, but the coffee and tea were free. During our stay I made all of the coffee and tea, determined to gain some value from this moldy palace.

After showering and taking naps we ventured out again and shared a pizza, only to return to our room, too tired to shop or sight see any longer. Conversation centered around the sad fact that we were spending more time in our hotel room than seeing the city.

"Whenever I think of Rome, I'll remember these moldy walls," said Steph.

"I don't think my feet have ever been this sore," I told her. "Every little bone is sore. It feels like a hundred bruises."

"I blame Positano. The steps there killed my feet."

"We have tickets to the Colleseum and Palantine Hill tomorrow," I reminded her. "Maybe we should just stay in and rest this evening and hopefully our feet and legs will be ready to walk again tomorrow."

"Sounds good to me."

We spent the evening in our hotel, reading and playing games on my phone and her Nintendo DS. We still hadn't located a voltage converter for the Nintendo so she had to be careful not to drain the battery.

The famous Roman pyramid

Chapter Two Hundred Thirty-Three
Roma
giovedí (Thursday)

In bocca al lupo.
Into the wolf's mouth.
(Good luck/break a leg.)

Response:
Crepi il lupo.
(May the wolf die.)

The night passed slowly, studded with the incessant sirens and horns, my feet unwilling to let me sleep. I read part of the book I'd downloaded on my phone, careful not to disturb Steph on the other side of the bed. For a while I forced my eyes closed in an attempt to rest despite myself, but dull stabs of pain in my feet and legs rendered sleep impossible.

Around 2:30 in the morning my phone dinged, indicating an incoming text message from Jason.

You awake? I read.

Yeah, can't sleep. I'm ready to come home.

My mom's in the hospital. This triggered my adrenaline—his mom is young and fit. My imagination raced through various possibilities as I typed a response.

What happened? Accident?

No. Her heart. Not sure what's going on.

Have you talked to her?

No. Only talked to Nicole. Jason's sister Nicole and his other two siblings lived near their mother in California; we only heard from them sporadically throughout the year and had no reason to believe his mother's heart was weak or compromised.

Call my sister if you need to book a plane ticket. She'll help you. I'll be home Friday evening so if you want me to go, I'll be ready.

Not buying a ticket yet. Waiting till I talk to Mom.

Keep me posted. I love you.

Love you too.

I lay there listening to my own heart beating in the dark room, wondering if we'd be flying to California the minute my feet touched American soil. Eventually the morning sun peeked between the curtains and forced us to greet the day.

Finally on this, the last day of our vacation, the palace redeemed itself through the rooftop breakfast buffet complete with an entire pot of coffee at each table. The buffet included the ubiquitous croissants and Nutella spread as well as fresh fruits, cereals, bagels and muffins. Determined to remain in our hotel until check-out time to rest as much as possible, we ate a leisurely breakfast and snapped photos of the city from various rooftop points.

Snooty McSnootpants had resumed his post at the front desk. He deigned to keep our bags once again, placing them in the storage area until we returned to claim them before boarding the train to the airport later in the evening. Sliding the bill across the counter, he drawled, "Your balance is 40 cents."

"Forty cents? I paid online before we left the States. I thought I'd paid in full."

"Apparently you made a phone call from your room. Each call is forty…cents."

"Oh, that must be for calling the airport to verify our flight."

"Regardless of…whom…you called, the charge is forty cents."

As I dug some coins from my pocket and placed forty cents on the counter, I asked, "Aren't local calls free? I thought the sign on the phone said all local calls are…free." I matched his conversational rhythm and smiled as if he were my best friend and I'd just traveled the world to see him.

He rolled his eyes, seeking guidance and patience from above. "The airport is not local. It is beyond the city limits."

"Oh, I see. What a petty little charge, then. Appropriately petty, I must say. It goes nicely with the…palace." With that, we strode through the gold doors to confront the city.

Every step brought sharp pain to my feet, shins and calves, causing me to walk like a crippled dog. I tried various walking styles: stepping lightly, shifting my weight to the outsides of my feet, smoothly rolling from heel to toe with each step and even tiptoeing, but nothing eased the pain. My feet felt as if I'd run a marathon in tight stilettos.

We shopped our way from the hotel to the Colosseum, pausing at market stalls and tourist shops to buy shoes, key chains, magnets, post cards, and we found a lovely little gelateria where the storekeeper took photos of us and chatted with us while we enjoyed double scoops of gelato. One of the stores even had a voltage converter, and although it was the last day of our trip, we bought it so we could recharge the Nintendo game for the flights home.

The Colosseum defies description, but my weak attempt yields words such as overwhelming and macabre. We explored every niche available to tourists and lingered in the gift shop before continuing on to the Forum and Palantine Hill, but our exhaustion had by then reached epic levels and prevented us from properly appreciating the spectacular sights.

Following a Rick Steves suggestion, we ate lunch in one of his recommended restaurants. It was a quiet place, blocking out most of the city commotion, and afforded us a somewhat energizing respite. After lunch we boarded a double-decker tour bus, ready to surrender to a crazy Roman driver rather than continue walking on our painful limbs. Our vantage point from the front of the upper level of the bus challenged our depth perception—it seemed likely we'd run over pedestrians or small cars at each turn—and we kept expecting to hear the crunch of metal or the screech of an injured person.

Our bus stopped in Vatican City near a few street markets hawking Roma shirts and sweatshirts. We hobbled off the bus and headed toward St. Peter's Basilica only to discover a line-up of over 500 people waiting to enter. Disheartened, we returned to the bus to reclaim our seats and finish the tour.

The rest of the day passed with dizzying speed as we rode and walked, viewing Rome's awesome marble statues, fountains and crumbling structures, incongruous amidst the modern buses and vans careening through the streets, accompanied by the constant chorus of horns and sirens.

Eventually we returned to the hotel to reclaim our luggage, staggering through the gold revolving door one last time to confront Mr. McSnootpants. I wondered if our appearance had deteriorated or improved since he'd first met us: we were more haggard, but less rumpled, than we were when we checked into his palace.

This time he communicated solely through disdainful facial expressions and pouty posture, practically tossing the bags at us before we asked for them. He must have anticipated our arrival, or had been watching for us on the street. We sat in the lobby for a moment, bracing ourselves for the heavy backpacks and making sure the straps were all tightened so the weight would sit as comfortably as possible on our small frames. We packed our newest purchases into the wheeled bags; everything we'd bought in Italy fit into our new bags, which would become our carry-ons for the plane ride home. Our backpacks, now with the expansion panel unzipped, would be our checked bags. If any luggage became lost at least we wouldn't lose anything new.

Suitably geared up, we left the palace to navigate our way to the Roma Termini station through the throngs of loiterers on the narrow sidewalks. We passed a beggar perched on a step, his skin hanging on his skeleton like laundry on a clothesline, cut-off shorts offering precious small coverage. Open sores oozed along his arms and chest. One hand clutched an empty booze bottle, the other a can for donations. Steph glanced back at me, clearly disturbed and sympathetic. "Keep going," I muttered, stepping around the spectacle.

Rick Steves warns travelers about the train from Roma Termini to the Leonardo da Vinci airport, stating clearly that it is at the end of the station. Even armed with this information, we were shocked to discover how far the end of the station is. Weighed down by our bags, moving with any speed is difficult at best but we had to speed walk or jog the entire way to make the train and avoid waiting for the next one, which wouldn't arrive for another hour. It started moving thirty seconds after we stepped into the car.

The train was full but we both managed to find seats on which to perch, resting our backpacks behind us so we wouldn't have to remove the straps. We held the wheeled bags on our laps. The ride was exceedingly uncomfortable and seemed twice as long as its thirty-minute length.

The Leonardo Da Vinci Airport is portrayed as a massive, confusing, poorly-organized terminal on many traveler website forums. Anyone traveling to or through this Roman hub should be forewarned about its inconvenient layout and location, beyond the city limits and requiring a train or high-priced taxi ride to reach. I'd read many warnings regarding this airport before purchasing our tickets for a 6:30 am flight, which required a 4:30 am arrival, which in turn made spending the night at the airport the only logical lodging choice. The trains quit running to the airport at 10:00 pm and the taxis from the city cost at least seventy Euros; if we stayed in a hotel, we'd have paid dearly for meager sleep (who can sleep when they know they'll be waking up at 3:30 to catch a cab?).

The one thing at the Leonardo Da Vinci Airport we weren't warned about in advance was the food. After we arrived and finally located the building in which we were allowed to stay the night, we realized we were hungry. The airport offered two choices: McDonald's or a cafeteria-style restaurant. We chose the cafeteria, reluctant to end our Italian culinary tour with an American fast-food restaurant.

We grabbed trays and pushed them along the counter in front of the large rectangular entrees and side dishes, none of which were labeled and many of which were unrecognizable, buried beneath layers of gelatinous gravies and sauces. The odors blended together to create a nauseating perfume. I ordered pasta with pesto and we never found out what Steph had—she gestured to the dish she wanted to try and the server didn't enlighten her with a name for it. We paid eleven Euros and sat at one of the tables, our stomachs now growling despite the disturbing odors and the slimy sheen on the pasta.

After three bites it was clear we were unable to eat our entrees, most likely prepared a few days prior and kept at a consistent lukewarm temperature that didn't quite stave off decay.

"I can't eat this, Mom," Steph looked like she was about to lose what little she'd swallowed. "I'm sorry."

"Don't worry about it. I can't eat this either. It's

slimy and crusty, and barely room temperature. It's making my stomach turn."

"Can we go to McDonald's? I'm starving."

"Absolutely. In this case, McDonald's is totally appropriate." We rarely visit fast food restaurants in the US, preferring higher quality food whenever possible, but I was confident McDonald's, in this case, was the highest quality attainable in that place at that time.

We wheeled our luggage carts over to the McDonalds and ordered French fries and chicken nuggets, a total of nine Euros, and settled at a counter with high stools to eat.

"This is the worst McDonald's food I've ever had," said Steph, visibly forcing herself to swallow.

"The fries are even bad," I agreed. "They must have been made yesterday."

"If I was blindfolded and told to taste this chicken nugget and identify it, I'd never guess that it's a chicken nugget."

"Who would have ever thought we'd be sitting in Italy, the land of awesome food, at a McDonald's because the 'real' restaurant was so awful we couldn't eat there, and then find out we can't even eat at McD's?"

"Yea, this is worse than that place in Venice with the TV dinners," Steph smiled thinly, clearly struggling to keep from regurgitating. I felt my own stomach revolting against this unacceptable food and gave up, tossing the remaining fries in the garbage and breathing deeply through my nose.

"Oh, guess what? I still have a bag of trail mix I bought in the Detroit airport on our way over here. I've been carrying it in my backpack this whole time," I foraged in my pack, holding up the bag triumphantly. "We're not going to starve after all!"

Steph shook her head and grinned. "Mo-om," she drawled. "You and your trail mix."

The night passed slowly as Steph napped off and on and I maintained a vigil, watching the bums camping out on the window ledge across the way and observing the families sleeping en masse, curled around each other and their luggage like puzzle pieces. The *polizia* strolled through the airport around 11:00 pm, a brigade of three sporting spiffy uniforms and shined shoes, one man casually spinning his rifle around on his shoulder strap. They roused travelers who weren't sleeping on their luggage, warning them of the possibility of theft or the illegal planting of items in their bags.

A small snack shop opened sometime past midnight, offering coffee, dry sandwiches and potato chips (plain or paprika flavored). The coffee tasted good and helped keep me alert. When I returned to our seats I nodded at the newest airport squatter, a George Kostanza lookalike who spoke no English but kept staring at us until I glanced at him, at which point he looked away every time. We were situated with no seats behind us so we could easily monitor everyone else on the floor and seats.

I played games on my phone and read the book I'd downloaded to pass the time and keep my mind engaged, frequently glancing around the entire room at the sleeping forms and George Kostanza. The airport is designed to deter any kind of rest or relaxation: armrests separate every seat, the floors are a clinical, cold tile, the lights are bright and the temperature is cool.

After 3:30 time seemed to catch up to itself, each minute passing quicker than the one before. At 4:30 we lugged our bags downstairs to the proper terminal and presented our air tickets at the counter, receiving our boarding passes and checking our bags through. I felt giddy from lack of sleep and kept cracking inane jokes, annoying the people working at the counters. By the time we boarded our flight my mind churned a nearly steady stream of incoherent images and phrases, most of which I managed to suppress before speaking aloud.

A stewardess approached us just after I'd drifted to sleep, inquiring if we'd like a beverage, and Steph nudged me awake to answer her. Exhausted and confused, I was unable to understand the question or keep my eyes open.

"Mom, are you on drugs?" Steph panicked.

"No, I'm sleeping," I answered, unable to focus my eyes and letting them slam closed. I realize now I must have felt I could finally relax on the airplane and rest, secure and comfortable since we'd managed to board the correct flight and had no other tasks to perform or maps to navigate.

The Amsterdam airport bustled with activity, travelers speed-walking the concourse and pausing in stores and restaurants for a magazine or cup of coffee. After going through security we chose some water and juice for our next flight, scheduled to leave in an hour, but the clerk changed our plans.

"You still have to go through another security check," she said.

"Another? We just went through it down the hall there," I explained. The clerk shrugged, uninterested in defending her remark. We bought the beverages anyway, intending to drink them before boarding the plane.

The scene at the terminal corroborated the clerk's statement: a makeshift security station had been established and passengers stood around in clumps complaining about the additional security and wondering what prompted the measures. Eventually the security personnel started accepting passengers. We formed a ragged line and proceeded through one at a time, each person subject to a thoroughly personal pat-down and an equally thorough x-ray screening of all carry-on luggage.

"You have five sharp objects in here?" sang out one of the security screeners.

"Mom—they're talking to you," said Steph.

"What? You can go through my bag if you need to," I told them.

"Five sharp objects. Do you know what they are?"

"No, I can't imagine what they would be," I frantically searched my memory, unable to recall packing anything sharp in my bag.

Another security screener interrupted, "I know what they are—did you purchase wine bottle…"she searched for the word, pantomiming plugging up a bottle neck with a stopper.

"Stoppers! Yes, I bought 5 wine bottle stoppers at the beginning of our trip. All of my friends like wine," the screeners all chuckled at this. "Do you want to see them?"

"No, it's okay to purchase bottle stoppers. Next!"

Steph and I moved our bags over near a wall to avoid being stationed along the main traffic area and wait for our boarding call. A young couple crouched down with their computer, so Steph greeted them.

"Oh, hey there," the girl answered back. "We're trying to find out why they're doing an additional security screening here. They must have reason to believe there's a suspicious character on board or something." Her boyfriend stared intently at the screen, typing a few words every now and then before finally giving up and stowing his laptop in one of their bags.

He stuck out his hand to shake, "We're from Seattle—where are you from?"

"Michigan," answered Steph. "The Upper Peninsula."

"Cool," they nodded together. "So, where did you travel in Europe?"

Steph looked at me as she talked, "We started in Venezia, then Siena, Sorrento and Roma."

"Okay, so you were in Italy the whole time," the girl summed up. "We were in Barcelona and Switzerland. We just spent the night here in this airport, and we stayed one night in a train station," she laughed, nodding toward her boyfriend. "It's been a crazy trip because we didn't really have enough money to come over here but the deal was so good we couldn't pass it up. We stayed with his aunt and uncle for most of the trip so that didn't cost anything, but he lost his job so when we go back he's got to start applying everywhere."

"If you get a chance, go to Switzerland," the boyfriend said.

"It's magical," agreed the girl. "So, what are you bringing back from Italy? Any sausage or pepperoni? Cheese, chocolate? Leather?"

"My husband wanted some sausage or pepperoni but I found out you can't bring that back into the States," I said. "So we bought mementos, you know like wine bottle stoppers and shirts and leather purses. Oh, and chocolate."

"Yeah, Mom got pulled over at the security screening because they could see the pointy wine bottle stoppers in her bag," laughed Steph.

"Well, we have a bunch of meat hidden in our bags," the girl whispered.

"Meat sticks and jerky," added the boy. "We figure if they tell us we can't bring it, we'll just sit down and eat it all right there." They laughed together, proud of their small rebellion.

"I'm too nervous to do that," I said. The PA system cut off my sentence, instructing us in two languages to board the plane in an orderly fashion. We wished the young couple good luck with their embezzling scheme and approached the line, eager to be settled in our seats and moving closer to home.

My initial relief at stepping on American soil quickly changed to low-grade anxiety as the security guards started barking orders to proceed single file past the drug dog, who dutifully sniffed every passenger and every bag. From there they herded us into a maze of crowd-control ropes eventually ending at the Customs Officers, intent on questioning every person entering the United States regardless of their citizenship. We searched for the Seattle couple, wondering if the drug dog was interested in their meat stash, but couldn't spot them in the massive clusters of people. "I hope they don't get caught," Steph remarked.

Each Customs Officer interviewed relatives together, so husbands and wives, or children and parents, approached the desk at once and were questioned and released as one. The elderly Chinese couple in front of us didn't speak English and didn't realize they were supposed to approach the counter together, so they each approached a separate Officer. Steph and I watched the drama, waiting for the Officers to realize the couple was traveling together.

"Where do you live? Your house," the Officer drew a house in the air with his fingers as his baritone voice grew in volume, drawing the attention of the crowded travelers. "Where is your house? In the USA?"

"I have house in USA," the rabbity woman yelled back. "I have house in China."

"You have a house in both countries?" He held up two fingers as the woman nodded nervously. "Which one is your main house? Where do you spend most of your time?" He tapped his wrist as if checking the time.

"I live China, I live USA," stated the woman.

Meanwhile, the husband was answering similar questions from another Customs Officer six feet away. Suddenly the Officers heard each other and ushered the couple to a senior officer before one turned to greet us and wave us forward.

"Where were you traveling?" He demanded.

"In Italy." I saw his nametag read Tim—it must have been short for Intimidation.

"How long were you there?"

"Two weeks."

"Why did you go to Italy?"

"Um…we just wanted to go there. No reason," I felt my face growing warm.

"Did you meet anyone in Italy?"

"Well, we met my friend Siw and her daughter Susanne. They're from Norway." This sounded lame, even to me.

He abruptly moved his dead stare from the far wall to my face. "How do you know people in Norway?"

"Siw was our exchange student when I was a kid. Twenty-four years ago she lived with my family."

He narrowed his eyes. "And you kept track of each other all this time?"

"Yes, mainly through letters and now email. We communicate two or three times per year," I forced myself to breathe evenly.

"What are you bringing back from this

adventure of yours in Italy?"

"Oh, the regular stuff. We have magnets, wine bottle stoppers, purses, scarves."

"You expect me to believe you went to Italy and you didn't bring back some sort of meat? No salami? No pepperoni?"

"Well, my husband wanted me to bring back some salami but I heard it wasn't allowed so I didn't bother buying any." I held his gaze.

He stared an extra two beats and flared his nostrils. "Good choice. You're free to go." He stamped our passports and waved his next victim forward, cutting his eyes sideways at us. "Welcome back to America."

Uscita (oo-shee-tah): Exit

Chapter Three Hundred Seventy-Seven
USA

Prendere due piccioni con una fava.
To catch two pigeons with one fava bean.
(To kill two birds with one stone.)

Anyone who's ever visited Michigan's Upper Peninsula and witnessed the leisurely pace of our lives here, despite the necessary multiple income streams required to pay the heating bill, might deduce the contradictory nature of our vacations. Rather than vacationing at a peaceful retreat featuring a lake lined with leafy trees designed to counterbalance an action-filled existence, we Yoopers (people who live in the UP) frequently seek a frantic respite fraught with sound, motion and physical challenges such as walking ten miles per day on concrete.

We are all celebrities in our tiny Yooper towns by virtue of demographics: a remote location + a small population = everyone not only knows your name, they know where you're going when they meet you on the street. Turn signals are superfluous unless one is altering one's regular routine. At least as celebrities of a small Yooper town we don't have to worry about the paparazzi. If we're inappropriately dressed or wearing too much make-up this news will probably spark the gossip chain, but photographic evidence won't surface in the National Enquirer. In this case, 'inappropriately dressed' refers to a lack of flannel and/or waffle weave layers.

While this life of leisure and friendly co-existence with well-acquainted neighbors sounds Utopian, sometimes we must seek anonymity in the form of a visit to foreign location. Foreign being, of course, anyplace outside the UP.

The last leg of our trip is a four-hour-long drive from the airport to our house. This is our vacation cool-down, a transition from an adrenaline-filled journey to our slow, comfortable, familiar pace. Once we're home we can revert to leaving our doors unlocked, entering our friends' and neighbors' houses without knocking and kibitzing with the post office lady while retrieving our mail. This transitory drive is like a long, slow pressure relief as we shed our vacation selves and become authentic again. We become the people our neighbors already know we are.

I always enjoy the obscurity of mass transit, trundling along with a crowd of strangers, trading innocuous comments and compliments with people I'll never see again; it's soothing to be temporarily generic. But I wouldn't trade my small-town celebrity for big-city insignificance for all the leather in Italy.

Shortly after we returned home we spoke to Jason's mother and discovered her heart trouble was minor and didn't require any medical treatment and we were free to plan a leisurely trip to visit her rather than rushing out there for a hospital vigil.

I chatted with Dani nearly daily, monitoring her progress from afar. She'd landed a waitressing job and was settling into the local society quite tidily. The remote town where she now resided was about six times the size of De Tour Village and boasted many facilities we didn't have such as a medical clinic, a shopping district and several restaurants. The summer calendar is peppered with various festivals and events designed to lure tourists and keep the locals busy.

Three weeks after arriving home from Italy, I drove eight hours to Madison, Wisconsin to attend a writers' conference for two days. I sat across from another writer after the first day of the conference, enjoying an expensive Italian riposte in downtown Madison. We were discussing vacations, listing the places we'd each visited.

"The best part of a vacation, to me, is when it's over and you're home safe, looking at the photos and reliving the entire trip," she said. "Every time you look at them, it's like you're there again. And it always seems a little better than it really was at the time."

"I never thought about it that way before, but many memories work that way. Like when life was a lot harder than it is now, but when I look back at it from here, it doesn't seem so bad and I'm able to see the humor. There was definitely no humor when it was happening."

Viewing my Italian photos produces sharp recollections of moments complete with scents, sounds and feelings and I hope I return someday to the world's first tourist destination.

Finishing my second book, a novel about growing up in Michigan's Upper Peninsula in the 1980s, before tackling the story of our Italian vacation was a daunting challenge. The euphoria of a successful vacation, and my desire to write this book, intruded on my daily thoughts. Steph and I still used a few Italian words such as *buon giorno* and *grazie*, and she and Dani called each other *sorella,* or sister, whenever they spoke on the phone.

Writing about our trip proved more difficult than I'd anticipated, largely due to myriad demands on my time and energy. After sending off my second book, I was promoted at work from a dull office position to an interesting field engineering position with a steep learning curve that required nearly fifty hours per week to maintain. We vacationed in Alaska for two weeks in August, visiting Dani and the rest of our family there (she was becoming a true Alaskan, wearing her Xtra Tuff boots and sporting a streak of pink in her hair).

In October a severe storm hit our end of the Upper Peninsula causing widespread power outages, which meant working eighty-plus hours that week. Every time I sat down to work on this book it seemed something else commandeered my attention, pushing my progress ever farther out.

Today, almost exactly one year after meeting Kate and Liam in Siena, we are driving across Nebraska en route to Denver. Phrases like 'waves of grain' and 'fruited plain' sift through my thoughts as I watch fields float past the window, windmills and power transmission lines providing the only visual relief from forlorn cornstalk stumps shorn the previous fall. The Great Plains stretch the eye, extending beyond the Colorado border, and I strain for a glimpse of the Rocky Mountains. Our conversation centers around how long it will take to see buildings and mountains, and how far the plains can possibly reach. We're tired and hungry and cramped after travelling for a day and a half.

Suddenly Denver rises before us to fill our windshield and our physical discomforts are forgotten. After refreshing in our hotel, we easily find Kate's house, one in a row of brick bungalows on a residential Denver street. Liam bounces out of the house to greet us, the same yet taller, a bit shy for the first thirty seconds, still full of energy and wit.

Kate stands in the doorway to usher us in with her trademark smile. "You look great! I love your hair! Steph, you look so cute. You must be Jason," she hugs me and Steph, and reaches out to shake Jason's hand. "I'm Kate. Would you like a tour of the house?"

We follow Kate through the house as she explains, "in the 20s or 30s, there was a huge fire here so they passed a law and from then on all houses in Denver must be made of brick. Some of the houses in town feature very elaborate designs with really elegant brickwork. I've taken photos of the more impressive ones I've seen."

She gestures toward another room with crimson walls. "That's Milan red," she explains as she leads us in a different direction, passing by several travel post cards pinned on the wall. "I haven't been to all of these places yet, but the photos are just so pretty I want them out where I can see them."

After the tour Liam showed Jason a new card trick and demonstrated the moonwalk and a few LaCrosse moves while we relaxed on the couch with a glass of wine and filled in the blanks of the past year for each other.

I'd forgotten how we'd clicked in Italy until we were chatting, discussing our mutual interest in architecture and design and, of course, travel.

"What are you reading right now?"

"*Cutting for Stone*," I answered.

"So am I! It's right next to my bed. What are your plans while you're here? What do you want to see?"

"We plan on going to Pike's Peak and the Garden of the Gods, and we want to see the city itself. The Tattered Cover is on my list, maybe the zoo, and the Rocky Mountain National Park if we have time."

"Hold on, let me write this down. Let's figure out a schedule for you," Kate hopped up and grabbed a pad of paper.

"I can see why you two get along so well," Jason grinned.

Kate returned and wrote up a loose schedule for us, filling our days with sights and adventures.

During our stay we discovered Denver shares

something with Venice: the San Marco Bell Tower. Denver has its own smaller-scale version downtown, called the Daniels and Fisher Tower.

The Tattered Cover bookstore is large and airy, crammed floor-to-ceiling with books. There are books stacked along the edges of the stairs and on the stair landings, posing a challenge for uncoordinated compulsive readers. The vision of myself tripping and causing a cascade of tomes to follow me down the wide wood stairs prevented me from reading while ascending, so I took one step, read a few titles, took another step, read a few more, and progressed thus up the stairs like an invalid undergoing physical therapy. There are comfortable chairs staged throughout the store, inviting one to move in and curl up with a hot drink (also sold here) and a stack of books.

The Rocky Mountain National Park and its neighboring village, Estes Park, invited us to move right in. I was fascinated with the Stanley Hotel and the interesting tales of Mr. Stanley and all that he'd invented and built here in the wilderness, decades ahead of his own time.

We visited with Kate and Liam every day, planning for their visit to the UP in July and possibly another foreign vacation together. Kate prepared a fabulous meal for us one evening, featuring three different entrees and a dessert. "I'm famous for cooking way more than my guests are able to eat," she said, "which is nice for the guests because you get to choose. Tonight we have this awesome chicken Parmigiana, which guys usually love, Italian sausage marinara sauce with linguine, or cheese ravioli with butternut squash sauce."

Kate's homemade dinner provided the highlight of our vacation. Liam provided the entertainment.

"I hate Subarus," he said. "Think about it: Subaru backwards is U R A BUS. You are a bus? What *is* that? I'll tell you what it isn't. It isn't a Jeep."

"Do you like Jeeps?" I asked.

"Jeeps are the best vehicles there are. They are perfect and cool and just so awesome. I'm going to own a Jeep Rubicon soon."

Liam decorated Kate's poppy seed cake, our dessert, with canned whipped cream and fresh berries, and cleared the table when we'd finished eating. The conversation continued as we explored each others' interests and shared stories about our families and vacations we've enjoyed.

"My middle son is being transferred to Australia for five years," said Kate. "You should meet us over there in 2013."

I felt my spine align, suddenly alert as my travel bone shifted back into place. Despite the adrenaline already brewing, I spoke with a calm assurance as Jason nodded his agreement next to me.

"Sure, we can meet you there."

Appendix

Appendix Table of Contents

Travel Research Notebook	207
Travel Info Booklet	210
European Voltage Concerns	212
Miscellaneous Organizing Tips	213
Slapdash Glossary	215
Recipe: Puttanesca	216
Silly Lists	217
Budget	225
Italian Inventions	226
Fibonacci Sequence Explanation	227

Travel Research Notebook

The travel research notebook is essential for me to plan a trip. Not only do I have a place to jot down details and questions as they arise, I have a custom-made reference tool when I am ready to embark on a journey. The research notebook is a great place to list all possible sights to see along with cost and location information to make initial scheduling easier and to use when extra time is available due to a cancellation or other change in plans.

I use the Levenger Circa notebooks because the pages can be rearranged as needed, and I generally have a section for each part of the trip, such as: Budget, Map, Itinerary, Hotel Info, and a tab for each city. The beauty of these notebooks is their adaptability: you can add as many tabs as you need, or remove tabs if you discover you don't need them. Levenger also sells a paper punch, useful for converting photocopies or magazine pages to Circa pages and inserting them in the proper section. These beauties can be found at www.levenger.com (no, I'm not earning a commission; I wish I could!).

Under the Budget tab I list the cost of everything as I complete my research, including transportation, hotels, restaurants (an estimate) and shopping (again, an estimate). The trick to a successful vacation is to budget big--whatever you're planning to spend on shopping and eating, add another 15% to ensure you won't be caught short. I also round up the costs I gather for transportation and hotels to provide an additional cushion. I then divide my grand total by the number of paychecks I'll receive before takeoff to calculate the amount needed from each paycheck. I round that up again and save that amount. For example, if my target travel budget, with bare-bones costs, came out to $5100, I'd first add the additional 15% (5100 X 1.15) to get $5865. After counting the pay periods before the beginning of the trip, I'd calculate the amount to save per pay period: $5865 ÷ 30 pay periods = $195.50 per pay period. Rounding that figure up to $200 would yield $6000, which is what I settled on for my total budget.

For the Italy trip I had an extra tab for communication; I did a lot of research on how to learn Italian and purchased a CD and workbook so I'd arrive with a working knowledge of the basics. I was also concerned with communicating to my husband while we were over there, and ultimately took Rick Steves' advice regarding phone cards and dialing home from hotel phones. The phone cards worked out great and although they sometimes charged us for more minutes than we actually spoke, they were the most economical choice for calling home.

Another necessary section is a timeline or schedule for preparation. For a trip as complex as our trip to Italy, where I didn't want to waste one moment of travel time dealing with something I'd forgotten or failed to plan, I created a timeline in my notebook. For example, we needed to schedule passport applications, foreign currency exchange, we had to notify our medical insurance and our credit card companies, and we had to ensure all bills would be paid in our absence. Airplane tickets, hotel reservations and train tickets all had to be purchased and/or confirmed.

These items were all listed on the timeline and addressed as needed.

Once the travel research notebook is established and outfitted with its various tabs, you'll find yourself referring to it often to ensure you remembered to include certain details and considerations. The notebook should be small enough to be easily carried everywhere in a purse or tote bag, yet large enough to easily contain all of the information. I used the 'junior' size Circa, which is about 5.5"x8.5" and I found it perfect for my purposes.

Travel Info Booklet

Here's a sample page from my Travel Info Booklet, which helped remove some of the anxiety and confusion of landing in a foreign country. It's impossible to remember the details for each city and each transportation connection; figuring it out once and then referring to the booklet saved me time and money. You may discover you need more or less information than I did, but you can easily design your own booklet to meet your individual needs.

Venezia: Arrive March 27, Leave March 30

1. Go to train station to purchase tickets for March 30 to Firenze.
2. Find vending machine and buy international phone card.
3. Go to bus station and buy 72-hour passes, 33 Euros each, for ACTV buses and vaporetti.
4. Take ACTV bus to Piazzale Roma, then take #1 vaporetto to San Toma (25 min.) OR walk from Piazzale Roma (10 min.) to hotel.

HOTEL INFO:
Al Campaniel
S.Polo n.2889
in Calle del Campaniel
(Campo San Toma)
30125 Venezia, Italy Tel: (+39) 041 2750 749

Directions to hotel if walking from Piazzale

Roma:

It takes 10/15 minutes walking from Piazzale Roma and the railway station (if you have light luggage, seeing that there are bridges to cross).
From the railway station cross the bridge, and take the street next to the Church with the green dome, visible when you exit the station. Follow the blue signs 'Giunta Regionale del Veneto', crossing a second small bridge, going towards and past Campo dei Frari. Take the street the DERSUT cafe at its corner and reach Campo San Toma from where Calle del Campaniel starts. We are opposite the 'Vizivirtu' chocolate shop.

Things to do in Venice:

1. Go to Harry's Bar, 20 minutes' walk or take Vaporetta to San Marco Piazza.
2. Climb the Campanile (bell tower) @ San Marco for 8 Euros.
3. Rialto Market, 8-10 am every morning
4. Bridge of Sighs (tour Doge's Palace while here)
5. Have a pub crawl dinner
6. Tour the underground prison
7. Peggy Guggenheim museum
8. Tour Frari Church (near hotel)
9. Have lunch at a pizza place near the Accademia Bridge
10. Tour the Gardens of Garibaldi & Giardini

HOW TO LEAVE VENICE:

Take Train # 585 to Firenze. Leaves at 9:20 a.m., takes 3 hours. €22.

OR

Train #9405 @ 8.27 a.m. to Firenze, takes only 2 hours, costs €42.

European Voltage Concerns

The 64,000 Euro Question: Adaptor or Converter?

We wasted lots of time and energy searching for a voltage converter, but it's not too late to save yourself! Find out before you go if you'll need one (check your child's bag for rogue electronic devices) and order one from the internet before you leave the US.

Here's an easy way to tell whether or not you need an adaptor or a converter for a particular electronic device: most devices state the voltage they can handle somewhere on the back or bottom, or on the plug itself. If it says it can handle 110-250 volts, all you need is an adaptor, which adapts the shape of the outlet from a US to a European style outlet (and there are several types over there, depending which country you're visiting).

If your particular device says it can only handle 110 or 125 volts, you need a converter which actually converts the voltage from 240 or 250 to 110 or 125 so your device doesn't burn up. Converters are more expensive but can easily be found on the internet and I would suggest buying them before your trip so you won't waste precious shopping time searching for such a mundane item!

Miscellaneous Organizing Tips

Organizing Money

It's cheaper to exchange enough cash to make it through the entire trip and avoid foreign ATMs altogether. In Italy, most hotels offer discounts for cash payment; some don't even accept credit cards, so cash is really the only option. I used paperclips and clipped the proper amount for each city and each hotel together to ensure I wouldn't over-spend in any one place. This worked out great and next time I'll take more cash with me so I won't have to deal with the ATMs. They worked, but the fees were quite high.

Oh, and spend all you take--it costs to exchange it back to US dollars when you return so you end up paying twice for the money you didn't spend on vacation.

Which Purse To Carry?

After reading about travelers' troubles with pickpockets I decided to purchase a PacSafe product. Their products are designed to foil thieves and prevent pickpockets and purse snatchers from absconding with your money and possessions. The purse I chose was comfortable, large enough to accommodate my Rick Steves guide book, passport and camera as well as money and keys, and it gave me peace of mind. I have used it to travel other places as well because it's made of microfiber so it is somewhat water resistant and is very tough--I never have to worry about my purse getting scuffed or scratched while I'm traveling. Check out the products at www.pacsafe.com.

Maps

Maps are becoming passe with the advent of GPS devices, especially those found on cell phones, but maps are still important on a trip such as ours. I had a simple map of each city as well as the maps in my guidebook, and they saved us lots of time and helped us avoid backtracking.

Slapdash Glossary

I can't compete with Rick Steves' phrase book, and I won't try. This list of Italian words represents the words we used or heard most often, and the words we found most helpful throughout our trip. A phrase book really is indispensable and I highly recommend the one Rick Steves sells on his website. It's well organized and is sized to fit in a pocket or purse.

Parla Inglese? Do you speak English?
Quanto costa? How much does it cost?
Aperto Open
Dove toilet? Where is the bathroom?
Chiuso Closed
Buon giorno. Good day (have a good day).
Ciao, bella. Hello, beautiful.
Buona sera. Good evening.
Per favore Please
Sconto (on signs) Discount/Sale
Scarpa/Scarpi Shoe/Shoes
Borsa Purse
Aperto Open
Chiuso Closed
Uscita Exit
Ciao Hello/Goodbye
Per Favore Please
Grazie Thank you
Mi Scusi Excuse me
Mi dispiace I'm sorry
domenica Sunday
lunedi Monday
martedi Tuesday
mercoledi Wednesday
giovedi Thursday
venerdi Friday
sabato Saturday

Authentic Puttanesca

2 TBLS extra-virgin olive oil
5 cloves garlic, coarsely chopped
1 tin flat anchovy fillets, drained, optional
1 tsp crushed red pepper flakes
20 oil-cured Kalamata olives, pitted, coarsely chopped
3 tablespoons capers *(I use the large ones, usually cheaper, and they look nice with the chunky tomatoes)*
1 (32-ounce) can chunky style crushed tomatoes
1 (14.5-ounce) can diced tomatoes, drained
black pepper to taste
1/4 cup flat leaf parsley, chopped
1 pound spaghetti, cooked as directed on package
Grated Parmesan (optional)

Heat a large skillet over medium heat and add oil, garlic, anchovies, and crushed pepper. Saute mixture until anchovies melt into oil and completely dissolve and garlic is tender, about 3 minutes. Add remaining ingredients. Bring sauce to a bubble, reduce heat, and simmer 8 to 10 minutes.

Toss sauce with cooked pasta and serve. Buon Appetito!

Silly Lists

Part of the fun for Steph and me was noticing the differences and comparing life in Italy to our life in Michigan's Upper Peninsula. Here is a sampling of some of the lists we made to pass time and acknowledge our fleeting homesickness while relaxing in the evenings.

List of Bests and Worsts

Best meal:
(Steph): Rigatoni alla zozonne in Siena
(Jan): Spaghetti Puttanesca in Siena

Best dessert:
(both): Tiramisu in Roma

Best snack:
(both): gelato, all flavors

Best day:
Two days tied for best day for both of us: the day spent exploring Positano and the day spent in Pompeii and Roma with Kate and Liam. The second-best day, we agreed, was the day we stayed in Siena, shopping and cruising through the street market.

Worst day:
(both): the day we rode the trains from Siena to Sorrento

A List of Annoying Things About Italy:

1. People—they're pushy, loud, and there are too many
2. Coffee—it tastes good, but the servings are too small
3. Traffic—too many cars
4. Language—difficult to understand
5. Bread—how old is it? How many people have handled it? Is it petrified?
6. Prices—high!
7. Streets—crowded!

Aaah, it felt good to acknowledge these things and write them down. After creating this list our patience expanded to allow us to laugh at these annoyances.

Italian Impressions, Alphabetized

A: Amalfi; ancient; awesome
B: bar; buon giorno; beaches
C: crowded spaces; caffe; ceramics; ciao
D: duomo
E: Euros; exhaustion
F: friends; Firenze; feeling foreign
G: gelato; glass (sea glass, Murano glass, stained glass)
H: homeless (people in Roma)
I: Italiano; itty bitty cars
J: juice (ie, fresh-squeezed blood orange juice)
K: kids: small and loud
L: language; limoncello; leather
M: masks; magnets; mopeds; markets
N: narrow streets
O: old; oranges; olives
P: pushy people; pizza; pasta; palm trees
Q: quiet (and the absence of same)
R: rain
S: Siena; Siw & Susanne; San Jimmy; smile (smee-lay)
T: traghetto; trattoria; translator; Tabachi
U: Uffizi; umbrellas
V: Venezia; vertigo; vertical towns; Volterra
W: winding streets; walking, walking, walking
X: hmm…nothing begins with 'x'…
Y: yellow lemons
Z: zesty life

Time Spent on Transportation:

Planes: 22 hours, 15 minutes
Waiting in airports: 19 hours (counting the overnight in Roma)

Trains: 12 hours, 5 minutes
Waiting for train connections: 3 hours

Taxis: 10 minutes

Car (rental in Tuscany): 2 hours, 30 minutes
Car (driving to and from airport at home): 8 hours

Bus: 5 hours, 50 minutes

Ferry: 1 hour, 10 minutes

List of Things We Missed About the USA While We Were in Italy:

1. Drinking smoothies (Steph).
2. Drinking extra large coffees (Jan).
3. Driving! Specifically, driving a four-door truck on a wide road with generous shoulders and ditches, lined with signs written in English.
4. Listening to English-speaking radio & TV
5. Enjoying the orderly flow of traffic without horns and sirens.
6. Drinking tap water.
7. Sleeping in our own beds.

List of Things We Missed About Italy After Returning to the USA:

1. Product prices in Italy are totals—no taxes or fees are added at the cash register.
2. The food (even anchovies taste good over there)
3. The language (It's no mental exercise to listen to English; in Italy the language provided an ongoing challenge to decipher and add to my vocabulary. And, it sounds prettier.)
4. The statues, architecture and general atmosphere of historical reverence
5. Street markets
6. Rome's sirens
7. Chocolate
8. Gelato

List of Places We'll Go on Our Next Trip to Italy:

1. Guggenheim Museum in Venezia
2. Campanile in Venezia (next time we'll beat the crowds)
3. Pisa's Leaning Tower
4. Cinque Terre
5. Roma's Borghese Gardens
6. St. Peter's Basilica
7. Orvieto
8. Uffizi and Accademia in Firenze

BUDGET

It's an ugly word, I know, but don't think of it as an indicator of whether or not you can afford a vacation. Think of it as an indicator of *when* you will be able to afford it.

These are the actual figures from our vacation, for which I'd budgeted $6000. I converted the prices back to US dollars using the exchange rate at which I'd purchased the Euros.

Food: $1125.76 (includes a gelato expense of $42.23)

Lodging: $1427.44

Transportation: $2190.94 (airfare, trains and buses within Italia)

Sightseeing: $229.60

Shopping: $1209.76 (clothes, purses, phone cards and tips)

GRAND TOTAL: **$6183.50** ($183.50, or 3%, over budget)

Italian Inventions

Take a moment to consider the impact Italians have made on our daily lives. This list contains a few items and systems invented by Italians (to list them all would require another book).

- Anemometer
- Barometer
- Battery (to store electricity)
- Coffee Maker
- Cologne
- Confetti
- Decompression Chamber
- Double-entry Bookkeeping System
- Espresso Machine
- Eyeglasses
- Fax
- Gelato
- Induction Motor
- Internal Combustion Engine
- Nuclear Reactor
- Nitroglycerin
- Piano
- Pizza
- Pasta
- Scissors
- Thermometer
- Violin

Fibonacci Sequence

The secret to the Fibonacci Sequence is easy: simply add the previous two numbers to calculate the next number, with the first two numbers being zero and one. Look back on the chapter numbers and check my math—the sequence should progress thus:

0, 1, 1, 2, 3, 5, 8, 13, 21, 34, 55, 89, 144, 233, 377 and so on.

Acknowledgements

Thank you once again to my stellar editing staff, each of whom is willing to work for less than peanuts and provides invaluable feedback to help me stay motivated long enough to finish a project. Without these esteemed friends, the average reader would find numerous errors and omissions (if you're a reader who has found one, this proves you're way above average). The list runs thus (in alphabetical order, still the only fair way to do this): Danielle & Stephanie Leazier, Angie Leonard, Jen Postula and Anne Stafford. Thank you, again, thank you, thank you.

Jan Stafford Kellis works full time at an electric utility company and helps her husband manage Kellis Construction. She splits her free time between reading, writing, luxury camping and of course, traveling. She's currently working on a new book project, maintaining a blog with random updates and planning her next major vacation. See www.jankellis.com for the latest news.

Ciao!

Made in the USA
Charleston, SC
07 May 2012